D0905099

Patrick Casement

On
Learning
from the Patient

Tavistock Publications

London and New York

First published in 1985 by
Tavistock Publications Ltd
11 New Fetter Lane, London EC4P 4EE

Published in the USA by
Tavistock Publications
in association with Methuen, Inc.
733 Third Avenue, New York, NY 10017

© 1985 Patrick Casement

Phototypeset by Saxon Printing Ltd, Derby.
Printed in Great Britain by
Richard Clay (The Chaucer Press) Ltd, Bungay, Suffolk.

All rights reserved. No part of this book may be reprinted or reproduced or
utilized in any form or by any electronic, mechanical or other means, now known
or hereafter invented, including photocopying and recording, or in any
information storage or retrieval system, without permission in writing from the
publishers.

British Library Cataloguing in Publication Data

Casement, Patrick
    On learning from the patient.
    1. Psychoanalysis   2. Psychotherapist and patient
    I. Title
    616.89'17'023   RC504

ISBN 0-422-79190-3
ISBN 0-422-79200-4 Pbk

Library of Congress Cataloging in Publication Data

    Bibliography: p.
    Includes indexes.
    1. Psychotherapist and patient.   2. Countertrans-
ference (Psychology)   I. Title [DNLM: 1. Psychotherapy.
2. Physician-Patient Relations. WM 420 C33750]
RC480.8.C38   1985   616.89'14   84-16281
ISBN 0-422-79190-3
ISBN 0-422-79200-4 (ppk.)

To
the many who
have helped me to learn

Contents

Acknowledgements

I am indebted to Arthur Hyatt Williams, whose enthusiasm first prompted me to start writing this book; to many colleagues and friends, who provided me with the stimulus to persevere and gave me valuable criticism throughout the writing of it; to David Tuckett for his advice on the final revision and to Gill Hinshelwood for her careful checking of the final manuscript. Above all, I wish to acknowledge my special gratitude to Josephine Klein, without whose patient encouragement and careful editing this book would never have been offered for publication, and to my family without whose forbearance it could never have been written.

Foreword

This book has much to offer analysts and therapists (whether students or experienced practitioners) and many others besides, such as doctors, social workers, counsellors and all those who wish to learn more about the psychodynamics of the helping relationship.

When I was asked to write this foreword I was happy about the task, as I remembered how interesting and fruitful an earlier clinical presentation by the author had been, in which he included details of his own work of internal supervision. That presentation, now included in this book as Chapter Five, was the embryo from which Mr Casement's book has developed.

Internal supervision is a process of self-review in the session. The author describes and demonstrates the value of this in many ways: for monitoring the therapeutic process, for helping to recognize how the patient may be seeing the therapist, for anticipating the implications of different possible interventions by the therapist, and for following the consequences of these. He then gives examples of using this aid to analytic listening to illuminate a wide range of clinical and technical issues, how to understand these more clearly and how to handle them.

There is a wealth of clinical illustration in this book, including some outstanding clinical episodes, all of which will be an invaluable source for learning or teaching psycho-therapy and for anyone involved in working psychodynamically with people in distress. The author includes examples of learning from mistakes, particularly his own. When a mistake has been made it can be brought into focus by a self-review on the part of the psychoanalyst, and a re-orientation is almost always possible. The compass of direction-finding in the mist of the psychoanalytic situation is, throughout, this process of internal supervision.

I was impressed by the way in which the author faced his own mistakes and evasions in the course of his internal supervision. The attributes that are needed in order to carry out such self-review are courage to face one's failures, mistakes and evasions (sometimes more painfully one's follies), devotion to the truth, scientific curiosity, respect for the patient and personal humility; while retaining enough self-confidence and indefatigability to carry on working. The author shows these attributes.

He also describes his own work with an unusual openness. This allows the reader an opportunity to witness something of how an analyst or therapist works, struggling with himself as well as with the patient, in the process of trying to understand and to use the different kinds of communication and emotional impact to which he is subjected in the course of therapeutic work.

It is a privilege to read the author's account of how he learned from his patients to refine his own ways of working with them. I did not know how much I had been affected by this book until I became aware that I, quite unconsciously, had begun to use these methods in my own psychoanalytical work.

The late Dr W.R. Bion said: 'I cannot help you with tomorrow's session. Only the patient can do that.' Mr Casement shows us that he works steadfastly along these lines.

Dr Arthur Hyatt Williams,
MD, MB, ChB, FRCPsych., DPM,
Director,
The London Clinic of Psycho-Analysis
12 April, 1984

Introduction

A number of observations have prompted me to write this book. For example, there is a common myth that the experienced analyst or therapist understands the patient swiftly and unerringly. Although some patients try to oppose this, risking the retort that they are 'resisting', other patients do expect it. Perhaps it satisfies a wish to find certainty. Some therapists also appear to expect it of themselves; perhaps to gratify an unacknowledged wish to be knowledgeable or powerful. It is not surprising, therefore, how often student therapists imagine that immediate understanding is required of them by patients and supervisors. This creates a pressure to know in order to appear competent. Interpretations offered to patients may then be taken 'off the peg', culled from the writings or teaching of others – who in turn have accepted such formulations as time-honoured, even though over-use rapidly degrades these insights into analytical clichés. I have therefore tried to suggest ways in which psychoanalytic insight can be rescued from this self-perpetuating cycle and discovered afresh with each patient.

Our creative learning from patients can be inhibited by the impression that everyone else seems to understand their patients so much better than we do, or is apparently less prone to being muddled, confused or caught up in making mistakes. It is my conviction that we can learn as much from our mistakes as from the times when we more readily get it right.

There have been some genius analysts, such as Freud and Winnicott, who learned naturally how to learn from their patients. It would, however, be inhibiting and misleading if others were to emulate either that genius or the brilliance of well-known writers on psychoanalysis. I believe that the majority of analysts and therapists are more ordinary, sincere hard workers – not necessarily brilliant – who seek the truth with such care as they are able. I count myself amongst those who strive to become better therapists with time and more experience, and I address myself especially to my fellow travellers in this quest.

The world of unconscious communication between people is strange and often awesome. It can also be complicated and confusing. This has led to a regrettable divide between specialists in the unconscious who have developed an esoteric language, with which they speak to each other more precisely, and the majority of non-specialists who feel excluded by this. I therefore wish to illustrate some of the dynamics of the unconscious mind, and of the helping relationship, in ways that I hope will be understandable to anyone in the related helping professions and to the interested lay reader.

There are some unquestioning believers in psychoanalytic circles; there are also sceptics in the real world outside. Amongst these, I think, are many who might have more respect for psychoanalytic ways of working if they could have a clearer sense of what it involves. These may be glad of an opportunity to follow some of what goes on in the mind of a therapist, as he struggles to get to know and to understand the complex mysteries of another person's mind and ways of being.

Opportunities for learning from the patient are there in all caring professions. It is mainly because the analytic consulting room offers a 'research space', within which we can best study the dynamics of this intimate interaction of the therapeutic relationship, that I address myself more directly to analysts and therapists. I hope, nevertheless, that those in allied caring professions will be able to play with the ideas I explore here and to relate them to their own spheres of work.

I have tried to share, as openly as feels tolerable, some of the difficulties which are commonly encountered in the extra-ordinary but challenging process of becoming a therapist and an analyst. It is my hope that others may learn from this too, and be encouraged.

Note
Some of the ethical issues arising from the use of clinical material from patients' therapy, and from students in supervision, are discussed in Appendix II.

1

Preliminary thoughts on learning from the patient

'However experienced we are we still know very little
indeed about how to bring up children, of whatever age.
We are beginning to know that we do not know – that is
something.'   (Bion 1975:147)

The helping relationship re-examined

There are many different caring professions, but the
psychodynamics of any helping relationship may be universal.
It is important, therefore, to become familiar with the ways in
which 'helper' and 'client' interact and communicate to each
other.

For this study I use the analytic consulting room as a setting
in which we can examine the therapeutic relationship, looking
in particular at the patient's perception and unconscious
monitoring of the therapist.

Many of the examples I give are from sessions with people
who were seen once or twice a week in analytic psychotherapy.
Most of these people (had they been differently referred)
could have found themselves with a social worker or counsel-
lor, a doctor or priest, or intermittently in a mental hospital.
Some of the work discussed was with patients who were seen
more than twice weekly; a few were seen five times a week. In
Chapter Two, example 2.4, I give a clinical illustration from
my own earlier experience as a social worker.

My focus throughout is more on technique than on theory.

But I do not wish to define or to prescribe ways of working which others should follow. Instead, I raise issues and questions, the answers to which will often lie in the work experience of the individual practitioner. From this, I hope others will also learn to learn from their patients, and to tune more finely their own technique to the changing needs of the individual patient.

For the ease of writing I shall not always refer to the therapist as 'him or her'. Instead, I will often use 'him' as a short-hand and other variants will be treated similarly. Likewise, I frequently use 'therapist' to stand for any professional helper who works psychodynamically. The exceptions are when I am referring specifically to a psychoanalyst seeing a patient in five-times-a-week analysis, or a social worker seeing a client.

Psychotherapy: a world of paradox

There are many paradoxes in psychotherapy. I will mention just a few.

For each person there are always two realities – external and internal. External reality is experienced in terms of the individual's internal reality, which in turn is shaped by past experience and a continuing tendency to see the present in terms of that past. Therapists, therefore, have to find ways of acknowledging both realities and the constant interplay between them.

There are many different ways of remembering. In everyday life, memory is usually thought of as conscious recall. When unconscious memory is operating another kind of remembering is sometimes encountered – vivid details of past experience being re-lived in the present. This repetition of the past is by no means confined to good times remembered, as in nostalgia. More often it is what has been fearful in the past that is re-experienced in the course of analysis or therapy. This is believed to be because of an unconscious search for mastery over those anxieties which had earlier been unmanageable.

Nobody can know his or her own unconscious without help from some other person. Repression maintains a resistance to what has been warded off from conscious awareness; and yet, clues to unconscious conflict still emerge in derivative forms which another person may be able to recognize. If this unconscious communication can be interpreted in a meaningful and tolerable way to a patient, what previously had been 'dealt with' solely by repression can begin to enter conscious awareness and become subject to conscious control or adaptation: 'Where id was, there ego shall be' (Freud 1933:80).

It is usual for therapists to see themselves as trying to understand the unconscious of the patient. What is not always acknowledged is that patients also read the unconscious of the therapist, knowingly or unknowingly. Therapists can no longer claim to be the blank screen or unblemished mirror, first advocated by Freud, because they too are people and no person can be blank or unblemished. Every analyst and therapist communicates far more to the patient about himself than is usually realized. It is important to take this clinical fact into account.

Therapists try not to make mistakes, or to get caught up in defensive behaviour of their own. There will, nevertheless, be occasions when this happens. Frequently, patients make unconscious use of these mistakes in ways that throw new light on the therapeutic process. The ensuing work with a patient is often enriched by the experience of the therapist being able to learn from the patient. In this way the therapy is restored from what might otherwise have become seriously disruptive.

In the course of this book I intend to show how I have come to deal with some of these issues in my everyday work, by formally developing a process of internal supervision, analysing from the patient's perspective what I think is happening. It is this process of internal supervision, and learning to listen, that I wish to share with the reader. I believe that this offers ways out of the many dilemmas that are inherent in psychotherapy.

Knowing and the use of not-knowing

Therapists sometimes have to tolerate extended periods during which they may feel ignorant and helpless. In this sense students are privileged: they have licence not to know, though many still succumb to pressures that prompt them to strive to appear certain, as if this were a mark of competence.

The experienced therapist or analyst, by contrast, has to make an effort to preserve an adequate state of not-knowing if he is to remain open to fresh understanding.

Bion, perhaps more than anyone, was explicit about the need for openness to the unknown in every individual. He did not advocate any comfort in knowing. Instead, he was clear about the anxiety with which analysts can react when they are genuinely faced by the unknown. He said: 'In every consulting room there ought to be two rather frightened people; the patient and the psycho-analyst. If they are not, one wonders why they are bothering to find out what everyone knows' (Bion 1974:13).

Analytic theories are built up to define more clearly the framework in which analysts and therapists work. These are necessary, if analytic interpretation is not to become a matter of inspired guesswork. Theory also helps to moderate the helplessness of not-knowing. But it remains important that this should be servant to the work of therapy and not its master.

Freud described the tendency towards dogma in his paper 'The Future of an Illusion': 'And thus a store of ideas is created, born from man's need to make his helplessness tolerable' (Freud 1927:18).

It is all too easy to equate not-knowing with ignorance. This can lead therapists to seek refuge in an illusion that they understand. But if they can bear the strain of not-knowing, they can learn that their competence as therapists includes a capacity to tolerate feeling ignorant or incompetent, and a willingness to wait (and to carry on waiting) until something genuinely relevant and meaningful begins to emerge. Only in this way is it possible to avoid the risk of imposing upon the patient the self-deception of premature understanding, which achieves nothing except to defend the therapist from the discomfort of knowing that he does not know.

By listening too readily to accepted theories, and to what they lead the practitioner to expect, it is easy to become deaf to the unexpected. When a therapist thinks that he can see signs of what is familiar to him, he can become blind to what is different and strange.

Similarity and sameness

It is a fact of the unconscious that, in any unfamiliar situation, elements that can be regarded as familiar are responded to as signs. They can be seen as warning signals, that a bad experience could be about to be repeated. They may also be seen as signs of security. Either way, the unknown is treated as if it were already known.

It is possible to see these responses in the phenomenon of transference. A patient is confronted by the unknown in the therapist, whom he seeks to know in order to lessen the anxiety of being in the presence of someone who remains unknown. The therapist will also sometimes react to the unfamiliarity of the patient in terms of what is already familiar. Everyone finds it easier to respond in this way – thinking that the unknown is already known and therefore can be understood – rather than to remain in a more prolonged state of not-knowing.

Bion encouraged analysts to hold together their knowing and not-knowing in what he called 'binocular vision' (Bion 1975:63-4). The analyst can learn to follow with one eye those aspects of a patient about which he knows he does not know, while keeping the other eye on whatever he feels he does know. There is a creative tension between this knowing and not knowing.

Sets, subsets and symmetry

When a therapist is confronted by unconscious communication from a patient, he will often encounter elements of primary-process thinking. It is necessary, therefore, to have ways of listening to this that will allow for the paradoxical logic of the unconscious.

In his book *The Unconscious as Infinite Sets* (1975), Matte Blanco[1] uses two concepts from the mathematics of set theory which elucidate in an interesting way these issues of similarity and sameness.

One concept is that of 'set', defined as a collection of all things that have a common element. So we can construe, for instance, a set of all cats. There can be a subset to this of all black cats. We can also, if we like, construe a set of all black things, with a subset of all black cats.

Another concept that Matte Blanco uses is that of 'unconscious symmetry'. This postulates a kind of logic which is basic to primary-process thinking. Unconsciously, we assume all relationships to be symmetrical. For instance, if John is angry with Mary, Mary is unconsciously experienced as also angry with John: they are linked by the relationship of anger. If John is to the left of Mary, in primary-process thinking Mary can equally be to the left of John: they are linked by the relationship of side-by-sideness. Similarly, if Mary is the mother of John, in this 'logic' of symmetry John can also be the mother of Mary: they are joined by the relationship of mother/child. The baby thus creates the mother who creates the baby, and vice versa. Likewise, the baby feeds the breast that feeds the baby.

There can be innumerable applications of symmetry in psychoanalytic listening, and in clinical experience. 'Self' and 'other' may be interchangeable, and this is true of patient and therapist. The part is often equated with the whole, the part-object with the whole-object. Similarly, 'inside' and 'outside' are frequently treated as the same. As Freud pointed out, in the unconscious there is neither negation nor contradiction. There is also no concept of time (Freud 1915:187).

Sets, transference and countertransference

If transference is considered in terms of unconscious sets, one can often identify what triggers this process. There is then an expectation that the present will be like a similar situation belonging to a previously formed unconscious set.

The sense of similarity, between past and present, can be initiated by either patient or therapist. Most often it has been thought of as the patient attributing elements of past experience to the therapist, or the therapeutic situation, and then responding to this as if the past had spilled into the present. It is, however, evident that the trigger for transference can also be unwittingly created by the therapist behaving in a way that echoes some aspect of the patient's past.

We could illustrate these phenomena diagrammatically by two circles *(Figure 1)*. If one circle is used to represent a set of 'present experience', and the other a set of 'past experience', anything in the area of overlap can be regarded as belonging

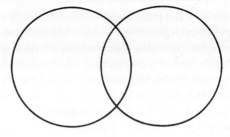

Figure 1

to either set. (This overlap may represent a similarity between the past and present of the patient, or of the therapist.)

From a conscious viewpoint, whatever the similarity may be, past and present can still be distinguished as different. However, because there is no sense of time in the unconscious, anything in the area of overlap can be seen unconsciously as belonging equally to the past or to the present. It is this mis-perception of similarity as sameness that brings about the phenomenon of transference, whereby previous experience and related feelings are transferred from the past and are experienced *as if* they were actually in the present. This is why the phenomenon of transference can have such a sense of reality and immediacy.

There may be a similar unconscious overlap between the experience of 'self' and 'other'. What comes from whom, in any two-person relationship, is not always clear. This is because the processes of communication can be either projective (one person putting into the other) or introjective (one person taking in from the other).

As well as responding to objective elements of similarity, patients also respond to their perception of external reality in terms of their changing inner states of feeling. For example, a patient may become aware of a growing dependence upon the therapist. This can evoke an unconscious set to which other experiences of dependence belong. The patient's internal reality (particularly in the clinical setting) may be seen to include additional elements being currently linked, such as feelings of dependence being associated with an actual separation pending. This can result in a more specific subset around that conjunction, evoking responses in the patient which duplicate earlier experiences of separation-at-times-of-dependence. These specific elements coming together in the present sometimes give an important indication of the particular time in a patient's life which is being re-lived in a transference experience.

This helps to explain why even a short break in the therapy, during a regression to more infantile dependence, is often more traumatic to a patient than a long holiday had been earlier in the therapy. Some people expect patients to be able to draw upon the fact of having coped during an earlier absence of the therapist. Clinical experience illustrates that patients are affected more by the current state of their inner reality than by their adult experiences, however recent.

This re-experiencing of the past is not necessarily confined to the analytic relationship. I shall first give an example of it occurring in a patient's home.

> Example 1.1
>
> A patient (Mrs P.) found herself crying in a distraught way after her four-year-old son had gone to bed. She could not think what had come over her. Her associations to this incident included the fact that her son had been very difficult earlier in the day. He would not do what she asked him. She had told him to go to his room, and when he refused she had screamed at him. He had then obeyed her and was no further trouble.
>
> Mrs P. thought that her crying had had something to do with this incident, but she wondered why it had upset her so much. It was particularly strange as her son had been quite all right later on. She wondered if it had to do with the fact that he had not been able to settle for the night until she suggested that he get into his father's bed, after which he had gone straight to sleep. It was only then, when she was on her own, that she had become so extremely upset.

Discussion: If we abstract the themes in this sequence we can see the triggers to the distraught crying more clearly. There was a mother/child relationship, with a child being difficult to handle and a mother screaming. Later, there were two people together in bed with the patient outside and crying. These particular elements could be regarded as belonging to familiar subsets, each related to unmanageable childhood experiences.

Mrs P.'s mother used to scream at her when she was difficult to deal with, after her brother had been born. Eventually, the patient had refused to eat – to the point where (at the age of four) her mother had sent her to a home until she recovered her 'correct weight'. The memories evoked by the coming together of these specific elements in the present included that of her brother being allowed to stay with her mother, here represented by the son allowed to be alone with his father.

The concepts of sets and symmetry can help us to see that the patient, as a screaming mother, evoked in herself an identification with her son as the child being screamed at. Secondly, the excluding relationship (which in childhood had been that of mother with brother) was being unconsciously experienced here as equivalent to the present relationship of husband with son. Each relationship combined the elements of parent/child and an experience of someone being excluded.

(This patient is referred to again in Chapter Six, example 6.4.)

Countertransference responses to the familiar

Therapists are trained to monitor their countertransference responses to a patient so that they do not respond inappropriately to a patient as to a 'transferential object'. (I discuss other aspects of countertransference in Chapter Four.)

I wish to suggest that, in one important respect, patients continue to be exposed to unacknowledged countertransference activity by the therapist. This is because therapists tend to develop an attitude (not unlike a transferential relationship) to their own theoretical orientation or clinical experience. As with transference, there is a tendency to experience a feeling of *déjà vu* when there are elements of similarity between a current clinical situation and others before it. This can prompt a therapist to respond to new clinical phenomena with a false sense of recognition, drawing upon established formulations for interpretation. The unconscious dynamics that contribute to this 'countertransference response to the familiar' include the therapist's anxiety, and a need to feel more secure, particularly when under stress with a patient. There is also a natural investment in one's own way of interpreting.

Example 1.2

In a series of clinical seminars, in which we were looking at 'failed cases', the following interchange between a therapist and patient was reported. A female patient had been in twice-a-week therapy for three months with a male student therapist. Clinical material was presented from the penultimate session before the therapist was due to go away for his Easter holiday.

> *Patient:* 'You will have to listen to me with extra care to-day because I have just been to the dentist. His drill slipped and he has hurt my tongue. It is difficult to talk.'
>
> *Therapist:* (relating this immediately to the pending break): 'I think you are afraid I will be careless with you; that I may not exercise enough care with you with regard to my Easter holiday, so that my words could bore holes in you and leave you feeling hurt when I have gone.'
>
> *Patient:* 'No, not at all.' (Silence.)
>
> *Therapist:* 'I think you are using the silence as a way of leaving me before I leave you.'
>
> *Patient:* 'No. In fact I was thinking of leaving therapy anyway. I think things are better. My outside relationships are better.'
>
> *Therapist:* (prompted by a recent seminar on ending therapy): 'Do you feel this improvement is due to work we have done together, or do you see this as your own achievement?'
>
> *Patient:* 'I see it as my own achievement.'

The therapist was able to persuade the patient to allow some time to think over this sudden decision to leave therapy. In the next session the patient told her therapist she had decided that she could not afford her therapy any more. She could spend the money she would save on a course for learning to teach English to foreigners.

Discussion: The patient began by telling the therapist there had been some kind of injury, which now made it difficult for her to speak to him or to make herself understood. The therapist did not appear to recognize any derivative communication in what the patient was saying to him. ('Derivative communication' is used to mean the indirect communication of thoughts or feelings unconsciously associated to, or derived from, whatever has primarily provoked them.)

The therapist listened mainly in terms of theory, and a premature assumption that this patient was referring to the pending holiday break. Even if this interpretation could have been correct in content, it was wrong in timing. By butting in here, the therapist leaves no space for the patient to experience what is described. By pre-empting the patient's possible anxiety about the therapist becoming careless, the therapist ironically then *becomes* careless.

Let us again abstract the themes. The therapist accepted the reference to a current carelessness as referring to the dentist. But, if we again think in terms of sets, the careless dentist belongs to a set of 'careless professionals' to which the therapist could also belong if he had been experienced recently as careless in the therapy.

By intervening too quickly, the therapist missed a chance of listening for further leads about an injury, to see whether this referred to him or not. There may be an allusion here to some recent interaction with the therapist in which the patient has felt hurt. If so, this could be making her experience the current difficulty in communicating with him. If he were to recognize the less obvious communication to him it would need special care in listening. The patient tells him so.

The therapist proceeds to relate the patient's opening statements to the holiday break. There is a clinical tradition for thinking of material before a holiday in terms of the break, but here it sounds rather bookish. The patient replies by disagreeing with the interpretation. The therapist responds to the ensuing silence with a further interpretation to do with the holiday break. The communication gap widens.

When the therapist does not understand the patient's allusion to something getting in the way of her communicating to him, even when she has pointed out that he will need to listen with special care, the patient considers terminating work with this therapist. She rubs his nose in this by saying her outside relationships are going better. A nuance here could suggest that these other relationships are going better than the present relationship inside the consulting room.

The therapist aims to assess the reality of this readiness for leaving. He thus moves into a new gear, which makes it obvious to the patient that he accepts her thought of leaving as virtually decided. The patient presses home her dissatisfaction. The improvement referred to feels like her own achievement, not a shared thing, nor thanks to the therapy. When the patient's decision to end is made final, she offers her therapist a parting comment which may contain the key to her feeling of injury. She is going to teach others to learn her own language (English). There is a sense in this sequence of the therapist having failed to learn her language. Instead he had imposed his therapy-language upon her, feeling prompted to do so by what seemed to be a familiar clinical situation. The traditional responses here, to do with holiday breaks or silences, are therefore not related to the more specific communications from this patient.

It is very easy to make this kind of mistake: and it is not only students who rely upon the understanding of others, and the knowledge of theory, to bolster a feeling of competence. Using a familiar element for orientation amongst the unfamiliar can be misleading, although it may bring some relief. In *Three Men in a Boat* (Jerome K. Jerome 1889), when the three companions were lost in Hampton Court maze one of them noticed that they had passed the same half-eaten bun before. This did not mean they knew where they were; it only demonstrated that they were going in some kind of a circle.

An exercise in interpretive re-orientation

As an analogy, the process of analytic listening and interpretive linking could be loosely compared with that of looking for a sequence in mathematics. The difference, of course, is that with patients we are dealing with human processes that are not susceptible to any such proof or disproof of accuracy.

Let us consider the following sequence:

$$- - 2 \ 2 \ 4 \ 4 - -$$

One response could be to interpret this as two pairs: *22 44*. We then have two numerical entities which can be linked by the multiple 2. Equally, however, they could be linked by the addition of 22. We do not yet have enough to go on, to know which sequence this belongs to. If it is the former we would expect to find the sequence to be extended, either before or after, as *11 22 44 88*. If it belongs to the latter we would expect it to be extended as *00 22 44 66*.

If these sequences were to represent clinical material, it would be a grossly premature interpretation to assume the relationship between 22 and 44 to be simply that of one number being twice the other. We need to be aware of the other possibility, so that we will wait for more of the sequence before trying to interpret. After waiting we can more confidently see which of these sequences is more probably being represented.

Let us add to the sequence:

$$1 \ 22 \ 44 \ 8$$

We can now eliminate one of the possibilities that had been previously considered; i.e. the sequence is not going to evolve as *00 22 44 66*. Instead, it looks as if it could be *(1)1 22 44 8(8)*; but it might still be premature to think we understand the sequence. For instance, the missing numbers in the sequence could turn out to be as follows:

$$61 \ 22 \ 44 \ 89$$

We would then have to abandon all assumptions we have made so far, being back in the area of not-knowing; and the sequence has to be returned to a state of apparent non-sense, as *6 1 2 2 4 4 8 9*.

If this were clinical material, once again we would have to listen to more of the sequence. We would also need to allow passive re-call of prior details which might contain elements of the same sequence. If we add to this now, before and after, we could have the following:

$$3 \ 6 \ 1 \ 2 \ 2 \ 4 \ 4 \ 8 \ 9 \ 6$$

At first sight this might look like a meaningless sequence of random numbers. However, if we look at it from a different viewpoint, we can discover that it makes sense if we rearrange it around a new axis. What had seemed to be non-sense will become meaningful if we break it up thus:

$$3 \quad 6 \quad 12 \quad 24 \quad 48 \quad 96$$

The above illustration, like any analogy, has its shortcomings. Of course no psychoanalytic listening can be so mechanical, nor should it be regarded as absolutely right or wrong. Nevertheless, the illustration does not represent the clinical experience of discovery that follows when we realize that we have missed something essential, when our initial assumptions are not borne out by what follows later in the sequence — or what may have gone before (perhaps unnoticed).

Re-orientation in a session

When in a session with a patient it can be important to sustain a sense of not-knowing, beyond the initial impression of having understood. Often the patient will provide the missing factor(s) that can point to the unconscious meaning which hitherto had remained elusive. I will illustrate this from the work of a female therapist.

Example 1.3

A patient of twenty-five was in her second year of three-times-a-week therapy when she became pregnant. As the elder of two sisters she had longed for this, her younger sister already being married with a child.

During the first months of the pregnancy the patient had treasured the privacy of her personal secret. No-one knew about this except her husband, her GP, and her therapist. Her secrecy was important to her because she had suffered all her life from her mother's intrusive attempts to control every aspect of her existence. Her marriage had helped to establish a much needed separateness from this widowed mother; and the patient had chosen to live at a sufficient distance from her to limit the mother's tendency to interfere.

The patient had been carefully preserving this period of privacy concerning her pregnancy, for as long as this could be prevented from becoming public knowledge. She then came to a session in great distress. Her sister had just been to see her and had guessed she was pregnant. She had directly challenged the patient, who felt obliged to tell her. She was now so upset because her mother would have to be told too, and the timing of this had been forced upon her by circumstance.

Since the moment when her sister had asked about the pregnancy the patient had had a splitting headache. Her therapist interpreted this in terms of the patient's familiar anxiety that once again her mother could become an intrusive influence in her life. The patient agreed. She had hoped to have had at least another month before having to resume dealings with her mother. The pregnancy had been her first experience of real privacy from her mother's compulsive interference. Even her marriage had not been immune from that. Her headache continued to be very painful.

Silent reflection: The therapist was reminded, by the patient's allusion to the marriage, that there had been similar anxieties then. The patient had experienced her future husband as threatening to invade her. Having only just begun to win some mental and emotional space from her mother, the patient had become afraid she might be about to lose this to her husband; and her marriage could become just another version of being owned by someone else, unconsciously representing her mother.

When the therapist thought about this reference to the patient's marriage she felt prompted to re-orientate her listening around the issue of pregnancy. Until then, she had been regarding the headache as a symptomatic expression of the patient's fear of being taken over again more directly by her mother. She had not perceived this as an allusion to her un-born baby. This was already inside the patient's body. Could it be that the patient was unconsciously experiencing the baby as representing her mother taking her over from inside?

> The therapist offered a tentative interpretation. Could the patient be experiencing her baby as a threat, perhaps as an embodiment of her mother's invasiveness which previously she had been trying to combat externally?
>
> The patient was able to think around this for herself. Yes, she believed this could be true. She had been afraid of being invaded physically, and of being taken over emotionally, when she got married. The baby could be an even greater threat to her, on the same two counts. It was as if she could never get away from her mother, and she could not get away from her own pregnancy. She was afraid of damaging her baby by hating it as a representation of her mother.
>
> After a silence, the patient elaborated further: she said it felt like an unthinkable thought that she could hate her own baby. She added that perhaps her headache had been an expression of the conflict between her protective love for the baby and her life-long impulse to get away from anything threatening to invade her privacy. She continued to think aloud around this. For her, it was an entirely new discovery that she could have hostile feelings towards the baby she so much wanted.
>
> Later in the session she realized her headache had lifted for the first time in several days. She felt convinced that this conflict in her feelings about the baby had been the key to her headache, which both the therapist and she had been missing until then.

Discussion: As a result of following the patient's cues, it became possible for the therapist to recognize that the current conflict might have to do with the baby. It was as if her baby might represent a 'Trojan horse', by which all she had most feared from her mother could take her over – literally from within. The patient's subsequent realization that she could hate her baby, as well as love it, carried the conviction of discovery. It was after all her own; the thought had not been put into her by the therapist.

The patient would have been let down if her therapist had continued to work over the patient's more direct and conscious fears concerning her mother. Equally, if the therapist had interpreted earlier the likelihood of the patient having ambivalent feelings towards her baby, that insight (though true) would have been premature and persecutory to the patient. In this case the therapist's slowness allowed time and space for the patient to arrive at this realization for herself, in a way she could tolerate and make her own.

Insight offered or imposed?

When patients feel they are not being understood, it is not always easy for them to communicate this to someone whose professional claim is to know about these things. The patient may also encounter the ultimate and irrefutable reply, that if the patient does not know something consciously it is because the patient is unconscious of the alleged truth being offered by the analyst. But it is not always just offered. It is sometimes dogmatically stated; and even a patient's rejection of an interpretation can be invoked as proof of its truth, and as evidence of the patient's defensiveness in response to it.

The analyst or therapist, as an implicit prophet of the unconscious, has a position of power in these matters which he must handle with great caution. Some patients do not find it easy to stand up to a therapist. Nevertheless, because they cannot always be right, therapists need help from the patient's cues towards better understanding. These cues are most often oblique rather than direct, unconscious rather than conscious.

In trying to understand the patient, a therapist waits until he feels that he can recognize a thread of meaning that can be identified and interpreted. But, in this work of interpreting, how can therapists avoid imposing their own theoretical bias upon their patients? Bion advocated that an analyst should approach each session without desire, memory or understanding (Bion 1967a; also 1967b:143-45). The desire (for instance) to cure or to influence, the active remembering of the previous session, and the illusion of understanding in terms of what is theoretically familiar, all contend against the kind of openness to the patient's individuality that is the hallmark of psychoanalysis at its best.

Whose resistance?

When a patient fails to acknowledge some truth about himself, as presented by the therapist, or agrees verbally without any significant shift in his life or in the therapeutic relationship, it is common to regard this as due to unconscious resistance within the patient. It may be so; but sometimes it can be an indication that there is, in this lack of change, an unconscious cue to the therapist to re-assess his assumptions about the patient, his theory or his technique. There may be something the therapist has not yet recognized, or acknowledged, and the therapist can be resistant too. Listening for unconscious symmetry in the patient's communications can often help to indicate what it is that has been overlooked. Potential stalemate in a session may then lead on to renewed movement.

> Example 1.4
>
> At a clinical seminar a female therapist discussed some work involving a male patient who continually shouted. In presenting a session, the therapist demonstrated this shouting to the seminar group. We were told by the therapist that she had tried many times, and in many ways, to understand this behaviour in the therapy. So far, nothing had helped it to alter.
>
> When one member of the seminar group asked the therapist how she felt about being shouted at in this violent-sounding way, she replied: 'Well, one thing I know about myself is that I don't have difficulties with aggression or violence.'

Discussion: By listening to the interaction here in terms of symmetry, we could formulate that *someone* was failing to get through to *someone*. What we had been assuming, previously, was that the therapist had been failing to get through to the patient – hence no change. But the interaction took on a fresh perspective once we realized the patient could be failing to get through to the therapist. Perhaps the shouting was an attempt at achieving this.

We could also wonder whether the therapist was only able to cope with being with an aggressive (even violent) patient by shutting off a part of her own responsiveness. The group had felt far less comfortable about the shouting than the therapist. So, if the patient were trying to get through to the therapist (but was failing to do so) perhaps he was demonstrating exasperation, or despair of being heard, by shouting louder.

Having considered that the resistance producing the stale-mate might partly be coming from herself, the therapist reflected upon this and became more able to hear what previously she had been missing in her patient's com-munication. She later reported to the seminar group that the patient had quietened down. The patient was now feeling heard.

The issue of control

It is easy to rationalize that patients should not be allowed to control their own therapy, as if this might 'render the therapist impotent' – to use a familiar phrase. But if the therapist insists on controlling the entire therapy, might that not equally render the *patient* impotent? Sometimes, of course, a therapist has to stand firm with a patient. There are also times when a patient has to stand firm with the therapist, in the name of his or her own truth. Such occasions can be misunderstood if a therapist is anxious about being manipulated or controlled by the patient. This often indicates that a therapist is feeling under stress; in which case it is usually more fruitful to listen to the sense of pressure, as an unconscious communication from the patient, rather than to react to it prematurely around an issue of control.

The therapist's responsiveness to cues from the patient

Several patients have pointed out how they first became able to trust me through discovering that I was willing to learn from them. For some this may be how they first come to find a basic trust. Unless this is rooted in experience it can remain an insubstantial hope.

Example 1.5

Early in her analysis Mrs B. (who had been severely burned when she was eleven months old) was telling me that the continuing pain from this experience and the attendant memories were making her hair go grey. I began looking more closely at her hair (over the back of the couch) to see if I could see signs of this greying. When I could not see any trace of this, I wondered whether it was an invitation for me to be closer to the patient. Perhaps if I were *very* close to her I would be able to see *some* grey hairs. I began to explore this as an appeal for me to be closer, thinking (to myself) that the patient was trying some hysterical manipulation on me.

Mrs B. became very distressed. When I listened to her distress, which was a crying from deep inside, I realized I had completely missed the point. I had been looking for outward signs of going grey. When I listened more closely I was able to interpret quite differently. The patient had been trying to tell me about her *inside* world, in which the scars from her childhood experiences made her feel that she was growing prematurely old. Part of the problem was that her emotional scars were not visible. She and I were having to deal with those other scars which had not yet healed.

Discussion: Although I had hurt this patient by my misunderstanding, by my focusing on the outside (where others too had found their reassurance that she had recovered from the accident), I was given an opportunity to be guided by the patient to recover from my mistake. She gave me another chance. This time I was able to recognize what she had been trying to tell me, in her enigmatic reference to her greying hair, and it turned out to be an important moment in her analysis. Mrs B. frequently referred back to this occasion. She told me that this was when she had begun to believe she could risk some dependence upon me. I had let myself be guided by her, which meant I could learn from her.

After her accident, Mrs B. had felt that her mother no longer seemed able to respond to her cues, or to her needs, in the same way as before. It was therefore crucial to her that I was learning to follow the cues she gave to me; and this became the basis for much of what later emerged in her analysis.

(This patient is referred to again in Chapters Five and Seven.)

I have noticed that as I have learned more about psycho-analysis, and about being a therapist, I have also become able to learn more from my patients. This has made me wonder about the different quality of relating that has resulted from this.

With some patients I have had to rely much more upon what I already know from the theory of psychoanalysis, and what I have learned about analytic technique, for that is often how I find (or maintain) my role. With them I have gone more by the book than by intuition, and I have remained more classically the same. With other patients, particularly with those from whom I feel I have learned most, I have found myself becoming responsively different to each of them. What does this imply? Which group of patients might be said to have had the better analytic experience: those with whom I preserved myself more firmly the same, or those in response to whom I allowed myself to be moulded into a more individual analyst?[2]

I have no easy answers to these questions. I can only eliminate the obvious extremes. If firmness becomes rigidity, it offers a false security to analyst and patient alike. On the other hand, the opposite extreme of an unreflecting flexibility amounts to 'wild analysis' with serious risks of unresolved countertransference difficulties being acted out within what is meant to be a therapeutic relationship (see Chapter Three for an example of this).

There remains a type of analytic inter-relatedness, that can be seen more clearly in some analyses than in others, but which may be a factor in all. I am thinking here of certain parallels with the parent-child relationship, that is so often presented for sorting out in the course of an analysis. To illustrate this I shall briefly digress.

Analysis and the nursing triad

Growing children need their parents to be able to respond differently according to different developmental stages. For example, a mother has to learn her infant's language if she is to respond according to the varying needs of her baby. Some mothers develop more skill in this than others. This difference has many determinants. There is the mother's own experience of being mothered; this will have left a set of images of mothering in her mind. A mother-to-be also has her own innate potential for being a mother to her baby; this potential can either be realized, or it can be interfered with.

From reading Winnicott I have come to think in terms of a 'nursing triad', whereby the mother is emotionally held while she holds the baby. The biological father may be absent, but there needs to be someone in the new mother's life whose chief function is to be there to support the mother-and-baby as they begin to get to know each other. In particular the new mother needs to be believed in as capable of being a 'good enough mother' to her own baby (Winnicott 1958:245).

Where this holding of the mother (as mother to her baby) is absent, there can be serious disruptions of the subsequent mothering. If the mother feels undermined as mother she may begin to resent her baby, which can come to represent her sense of failure as a mother. (Society sometimes reinforces a mother's insecurities here, when attention is more often focused on the mother than upon those who have failed to give her the support she has needed.) This lack of confidence in herself can be aggravated by other people's readiness to tell her what to do, and by others taking over and seeming to be better mothers to her baby. There may also be an internal erosion of confidence from bad childhood experiences of being mothered, or (in the present) of not being believed in or supported as a mother. Added to that there is sometimes a persecutory awareness of the baby's failure to thrive or to feel secure in the mother's handling. All these factors can contribute to a tendency to neglect the baby, even to give in to impulses to attack a baby who represents an attack upon herself as a mother.

If, on the other hand, a mother feels adequately held (as mother to her baby) she is more able to learn from her baby how best to be the mother which, at that moment, her baby most needs her to be. To begin with, this means learning her baby's language and individual rhythms; and these will not be the same as in the books, or the same as the baby next door, or the average baby that some child experts seem to speak of (with their 'milestones' and so on). These will also not be the same as in the case of any other baby that the mother previously may have had. Each baby is different.

A mother who thus allows herself to respond to the individuality of each of her babies will, in some measure, find herself being a different mother to each. She will also find herself changing with time, through her continuing to learn from her baby/child in response to changing developmental needs (Winnicott 1965b:Chapter 7).

The father (or father substitute) comes into this too. From the beginning that holding presence is of crucial importance to the mother, and the child benefits or suffers according to the quality of that support. The 'father' later comes into a different role, as the child moves into discovering about triangular relationships. Still later the adolescent presents different needs again, requiring a firmness which 'belongs to containment that is non-retaliatory, without vindictiveness, but having its own strength' (Winnicott 1971:Chapter 11).

The patient, the analyst and the internal supervisor

I have covered the above, familiar, ground in some detail as I believe that similar dynamics apply in the analytic relationship. We can see this most clearly in relation to students.

Student analysts and therapists have a particular need to be professionally held while they learn about the analytic holding that a patient needs in therapy. They should be able to draw upon the experience of their own analysis; they can also be held by their knowledge of theory and of technique, to have the security to continue to function analytically even under pressure. But, in addition, there needs to be a supervisory holding by an experienced person who believes in the student's potential to be in tune with the patient and to comment helpfully.

However, students need to be able to develop a style of working which is compatible with their own personality; so there will be something essential missing if he or she becomes too much of a *pastiche* of the training analyst, or the supervisor, however unconscious that may be.

Amongst the pitfalls of a supervisor (and here I draw upon what I have learned from those I have supervised) is the danger of offering too strong a model of how to treat the patient. This can mislead students into learning by a false process, borrowing too directly from a supervisor's way of working rather than developing their own. Some students can be seriously undermined in this way, feeling as if the treatment (or even the patient) has been taken over by the supervisor.

Here there are echoes of the mother who feels she is being told how to be a mother, and the results can be similarly disturbing to the student's analytic attitude towards the patient. For, if a patient comes to represent the student's difficulties in believing in himself as a therapist, he will have problems in working with that patient.

Winnicott was careful always to respect a mother's understanding of her own child. He therefore used to emphasize that he was only an expert on mothers and babies in general. Although he might be useful to a particular mother, it was she who continued to be acknowledged as the person who knew her own baby better than anyone else (Winnicott 1965a: Chapter 1).

As with the mother, this holding of the student therapist is first experienced as coming from outside. Transitionally the experience of supervision is usually internalized. Ultimately this needs to develop into an internal support that is autonomous and separate from the internalized supervisor. So, in order to emphasize this further development, I have come to think in terms of an internal supervisor (see Chapter Two).

When the internal supervisor remains poorly individuated there is a tendency for therapists to rely too much upon the thinking of others. But, any strong adherence to a particular school of theory, or position on technique, can itself become intrusive. The analytic process can easily become tilted in a pre-determined direction, which means it then ceases to be truly exploratory or psychoanalytic.

It is not surprising that the critics of psychoanalysis can point out how Freudian patients seem to have Freudian dreams, whereas Jungian or Kleinian patients are said to have dreams that fit in with the different theoretical position of *their* analysts. Here, I think, we have evidence of patients being taught to speak the language of the analyst; and not only language. Parallels may be found, among analysts and therapists, with mothers who assume they know best what their baby needs. We also hear of mothers who did not trust their own judgement sufficiently, having been misguided by authorities on child-rearing (Truby King among others) into believing they could bring up their babies by the book rather than 'by the baby'.

If 'the book' is given too much importance, then the choice of book becomes a crucial issue. Many bitter controversies might have been avoided if more analysts had questioned their belief in the over-riding importance of a fully integrated theory.[3] When analysts and therapists go rather more 'by the patient', and less by the particular theoretical orientation by which they feel supported, it becomes easier to notice when a patient feels out of tune with what is being said or with how the analysis is being conducted. Some patients may need a different style of analysis. It is important that therapists leave themselves room in their technique to allow for this. The analytic process becomes seriously restricted if therapists define themselves out of this possibility in the name of their own chosen orthodoxy.

In order to guard against the distorting influence of theoretical bias I find it useful to keep asking myself two questions, before and after interpreting or when supervising: (1) 'Is the patient's individuality being respected and preserved, or overlooked and intruded upon?'; (2) 'Who is putting what into the analytic space, at this moment, and why?'

Psychoanalysis has the potential for enabling a re-birth of the individual personality. It is a tragedy if this comes to be limited to a process nearer to that of 'cloning', whereby the patient comes to be 'formed in the image' of the analyst and his theoretical orientation.

Learning from the patient

In his book *Orthodoxy* (1908), G.K.Chesterton imagines:

'an English yachtsman who slightly miscalculated his course and discovered England under the impression that it was a new island in the South Seas... who landed (armed to the teeth and talking by signs) to plant the English flag on that barbaric temple which turned out to be the Pavilion at Brighton.'

(edition 1961:9)

If a therapist trusts in the analytic process he will often find himself led by the patient to where others have been before. The importance for the patient is that any theoretical similarity to what previously has been conceptualized in relation to others shall be arrived at through fresh discovery, not pre-conception.

The therapist's openness to the unknown in the patient leaves more room for the patient to contribute to any subsequent knowing; and what is thus jointly discovered has a freshness which belongs to both. More than this, it may be that a significant part of the process of therapeutic gain is achieved through the patient coming to recognize that the therapist can learn from him or her. The patient is thus given a real part to play in helping the therapist to help the patient and, to that end, to discover what is needed in that patient's therapy.

Patients benefit from a therapist's willingness to find out, even that which is already 'known', through working clinically with them. This feels better by far than using short-cuts to understanding, based on what is borrowed from others – and which patients also borrow. Fresh insight emerges more convincingly when a therapist is prepared to struggle to express himself within a patient's language, rather than falling back upon old thinking.

When I let patients play a part in how their therapy evolves I do not find myself being made helpless because of this. At times I may even have to become drawn into a 'harmonious mix-up' within the analytic relationship (Balint 1968). There are, of course, other times when I have to maintain an adequate firmness, without which a patient could feel insecure and deprived of the opportunity to experience confrontation with someone clearly separate and different from himself. For instance, when a patient is ready to find a therapist's otherness (or what Winnicott calls 'externality') the therapist has to be able to respond to the patient's attacks, upon him and the therapy, without collapse or retaliation (Winnicott 1971: Chapter 6).

Therapists need confidence in the analytic process if they are to be able to tolerate the vicissitudes of being used by their patients in these different ways. They need to be able to follow the patient, without feeling too much at sea to function analytically. For this they will need an adequate orientation to hold them near enough on course, or to help them back on course when they become lost.

In the treatment setting, it is a function of the internal supervisor to hold the analyst (or therapist) who is learning to hold the patient. This provides the structure of an internal 'nursing triad', which can help the therapist to find an inner play-space where the clinical options can be explored (silently or with the patient) rather than remaining blinkered by past thinking that often functions too much like a set of rules.

In the rest of this book I intend to examine various aspects of the interaction between a patient and the analyst or therapist. It is my belief that therapists could risk being less tenacious in their adherence to particular theoretical positions if they allowed themselves to be more receptively open to what their patients communicate to them at so many diverse levels.

When a therapist learns to follow the patient's cues, and listens to the resulting dialogue between the two viewpoints of 'binocular vision' (Bion 1975), of knowing and not-knowing, he will frequently find himself led towards the understanding which is needed.

Notes

1. I first heard of Matte Blanco's use of these concepts, unconscious symmetry and sets, in a paper presented to the British Psycho-Analytical Society in 1980, by Eric Rayner. A version of that paper has now been published: 'Infinite Experiences, Affects and the Characteristics of the Unconscious' (Rayner 1981).

2. Since writing this chapter, I have been pleased to find Sandler expressing similar thoughts in his paper 'Reflections on some Relations between Psychoanalytic Concepts and Psychoanalytic Practice.' In this he says:

> 'The conviction that what is actually done in the analytic consulting room is not "kosher", that colleagues would criticize it if they knew about it, comes from the reality that any analyst worth his salt will adapt to specific patients on the basis of his interaction with those patients. He will modify his approach so that he can get as good as possible a working analytic situation developing. To achieve this, he needs to feel relaxed and informal with his patient to an appropriate degree, and at times he might have to depart quite far from "standard" technique.'
>
> (Sandler 1983:38)

3. Sandler begins his paper (quoted above) by saying:

> 'If one looks carefully one can find an implicit unconscious assumption in many psychoanalytic writings that our theory should aim to be a body of ideas that is essentially complete and organized, with each part being fully integrated with every other.'

He later continues:

> 'There are advantages to emphasizing the developmental-historical dimension in psychoanalysis when we think of theoretical matters. It allows us to escape – if we want to – quarrels about which theory is "right" and which is "wrong". Rather, it puts us in the position of asking "Why was this, that or the other formulation put forward?" and "What did its authors mean?"'
>
> (Sandler 1983:35)

2

The internal supervisor

Internal supervision: a quest for balance

Therapists are often related to by the patient as a transferential object, representing aspects of earlier relationships, and yet also as a real object. This means that they have to be able to remain well disposed towards a patient even when they are being treated as someone with attitudes that may be quite alien.

In order that a patient can relate to the therapist, as freely as possible in terms of the patient's inner reality, it has long been accepted that the analytic process should be protected from needless interference from the therapist's own personality. However, in order to avoid becoming intrusive in the therapy, some therapists become defensive in trying to be as little in evidence as possible. Unfortunately, falling over backwards (in trying to achieve this) can become just as intrusive as falling forwards into the centre vision of the patient's awareness. As far as possible, the therapist's presence therefore has to remain a transitional or potential presence (like that of a mother who is non-intrusively present with her playing child). The therapist can then be invoked by the patient as a presence, or can be used by the patient as representing an absence.

This is the world of potential space (Winnicott 1971: Chapter 3) which is part real and part illusory, and here I use the notion of illusion as belonging to the experience of playing (ludo = to play). In this space the patient needs to be allowed opportunities for optimum experience, without interference from the therapist.

In order to preserve for the patient the creative potential of this space, therapists have to learn how to remain close enough to what the patient is experiencing for this to have a feeling impact upon himself while preserving a sufficient distance still to function as therapist. But that professional distance should not leave him beyond the reach of what the patient may need him to feel. A therapist has to discover how to be psycho-logically intimate with a patient and yet separate, separate and still intimate.

In their day-to-day functioning, therapists have to feel their way amidst many paradoxical pulls and pushes; and they have to acquire a sense of balance if they are to feel at ease in this therapeutic *pas de deux*. What is needed, therefore, is more than just those external aspects of the nursing triad referred to in the previous chapter.

Support from a supervisor or analyst can offer *hindsight* on what has been missed in an earlier session; it can also offer *foresight* in relation to what may be yet encountered. Therap-ists still need to develop a capacity to function with more immediate (but not instant) *insight* within the momentum of the analytic process. Not even that which is sometimes called the 'internalized supervisor' meets all that is required here.

As a counterbalance to the many pressures upon a therapist in a session, I have found it useful to think in terms of an internal supervisor (Casement 1973).[1] I first began to articu-late the need for this in supervising others. I noticed that trainees in supervision often lean too heavily upon the advice or comments of a supervisor, which creates a barrier between the social worker or therapist and the client or patient. The effect of this becomes evident in the trainee's subsequent clinical work. I therefore came to see that formal supervision alone does not adequately prepare a student to deal with the immediacy of the therapeutic present.

The development of an internal supervisor[2]

What I am calling the internal supervisor has origins that derive from before the experience of supervision and its development continues far beyond it. I shall trace this here with particular reference to therapists, as they are specifically required to have personal analysis as a part of their training. In other helping professions, all the other stages described here are similar.

During personal analysis

Writing from the point of view of an analyst seeing a patient, Sterba (1934) stresses that it is important to enable a 'therapeutic ego-dissociation' within the ego of the patient. This, he points out, is achieved by interpreting the transference. One result of this is that the patient is encouraged to observe with the analyst what he (the patient) is experiencing. The two aspects of this split have sometimes been referred to as the 'observing ego' and the 'experiencing ego'. In this paper, Sterba also introduces the notion of 'an island of intellectual contemplation'. So, when therapists have become genuinely involved in their own analysis, they too will have experienced this need to find within themselves (as patient) that island of contemplation – from which they could observe with their analyst what they were experiencing in the transference.

It is here, in their own experience of being a patient, that therapists establish the first roots of what later becomes the internal supervisor. Something is added to this in each phase of training and subsequent clinical work. As our experience grows, so we build on what has gone before.

Being supervised

This may be considered in three separate phases, as the function of supervision during the early stages of training is different from what is needed later.

(1) When therapists first begin to treat a patient they have limited resources to draw upon. They have what they know of theory. They have what so far has been experienced in their own analysis. They may also have some knowledge of the work of other people, as this has been written about or has been presented in clinical seminars.

However, the only direct experience of being in a therapeutic role that student therapists have had before is often in some other discipline, as a doctor or psychiatrist, as teacher or as social worker. At times, particularly when being stressed by a patient, there can be a strong pull to revert to type – calling upon earlier modes of functioning that are familiar. This can hinder a fuller learning of the new mode of functioning that is required of a student in becoming a therapist or an analyst.

Therefore, when a student therapist begins to work with training cases under supervision, the supervisor has a crucially important function in holding the student during this opening phase of clinical work – while he or she is learning to hold the patient analytically. The supervisor provides a form of control, making it safe for the therapist and patient to become analytically engaged, and helping a student to understand and to contain what is being presented by the patient. The foundations are laid down here for working independently later on.

At the outset, students naturally rely a good deal upon the advice and comments offered by the supervisor. With time, these supervisory insights should become more integrated into the on-going work with a patient. Sometimes, however, they continue to impinge upon this as elements of borrowed thinking.

(2) During the course of being supervised, therapists need to acquire their own capacity for spontaneous reflection within the session, alongside the internalized supervisor. They can thus learn to watch themselves as well as the patient, now using this island of intellectual contemplation as the mental space within which the internal supervisor can begin to operate.

(3) Towards the end of training, I believe that the process of supervision should develop into a dialogue between the external supervisor and the internal supervisor. It is through this that therapists develop the more autonomous functioning that is expected of them upon qualification.

Working without formal supervision

After therapists first qualify there is an important period of consolidation. In his teaching and supervising, John Klauber used to emphasize that it takes at least ten years to become an

analyst after being qualified. Bion stressed that 'becoming' is a
process which begins, continues, and is never completed. We
should always be in a state of becoming (Bion 1975:26). At the
time of qualifying, a more autonomous internal supervisor
may be forming in the therapist; but I hope there will never be
a time when therapists cease from this 'becoming' or imagine
that they have 'arrived'.

Supervising others

When therapists have an opportunity to supervise others, they
can enter into a further phase of growth that recapitulates
much of what has gone before. The sequence is like a spiral in
which they can find themselves back at a beginning, the
beginning of training or the beginning of a treatment. They
are back where they have been before, but also where they
have never been before.

Just as we can see our own errors more clearly in others, so
too in supervising others. Here there are endless opportunities for therapists to re-examine their own work, when looking
closely at the work of the person being supervised. Not
infrequently, supervisors will be seeing reflections of their
own difficulties with technique. We do not always do as we
teach others to do, but we can learn a lot by trying to do so.

When I have followed the work of my supervisees from an
interactional point of view[3] it has brought home to me how
closely patients follow the work of their therapists, monitoring
their moods, noticing their timing, wondering about the
unconscious implications of their comments (what clues these
may give the patient beyond the attempted inscrutability of
the therapist). I had not realized before how much I too must
give away of myself in the manner of my own interventions, or
the mode of my responses to a patient.

Renewed reflection

Once I had come to recognize this unintentional manoeuvring
of the patient by those I supervise, it became imperative for me
to monitor my own work more closely. Some therapists might
be surprised by how often they could be falling into modes of
intervention that they have questioned when supervising
someone else. This realization can stir into life a renewed cycle

of learning about technique, and about our own contribution to the responses that we see in our patients.

Trial identification

As a part of the internal supervision that I am suggesting, I often find it helpful to use trial identification (Fliess 1942). This can also be thought of as related to empathy in seeking to understand a patient. Reik (1937) pointed out that we develop empathy as a capacity to share in the experience of others, not just *like* our own but *as* our own.

Money-Kyrle linked this to the analyst's familiarity with his own unconscious:

> 'It is just because the analyst can recognize his early self which has already been analysed, in the patient, that he can analyse the patient. His empathy and insight, as distinct from his theoretical knowledge, depend on this kind of partial identification. Identification can take two forms – introjective and projective. We may therefore expect to find both forms in the analyst's partial identi-fication with his patient. As the patient speaks, the analyst will as it were become introjectively identified with him, and having understood him inside, will re-project him and interpret. What I think the analyst is most aware of is the projective phase – that is to say, the phase in which the patient is the representative of a former immature or ill part of himself, including his damaged objects, which he can now understand and therefore treat by interpretation, in the external world.'
>
> (Money-Kyrle 1956:360-61)

It is therefore not just the patient who needs to develop the capacity for a therapeutic dissocation within his ego, such as Sterba describes. The therapist also has to be able to maintain this benign split within himself, whereby his experiencing ego is free to move between himself and the patient, between thinking and feeling. Kris refers to this as 'regression in the service of the ego' (Kris 1950). The analyst uses a controlled regression within himself in order to cross the boundary between his conscious (rational) thinking and his unconscious (primary-process/irrational) thinking. Allowing himself this freedom to enter a state of listening reverie, alongside the patient, he can monitor what it may feel like to be the patient (in whichever context).

Now, when I use trial identification I do so in a number of different ways. I may, for example, think or feel myself into whatever experience is being described by a patient. I may also put myself into the shoes of the other person being referred to. From each of these viewpoints it is possible to pick up elements of the patient's object-relating that might otherwise be missed.

In addition to these more usual ways of monitoring a patient through trial identification, I also try to put myself into the patient's shoes in his or her relationship to me. I try to listen (as the patient might) to what it crosses my mind to say, silently trying out a possible comment or interpretation. This helps me to recognize when a patient could mis-hear what I wish to say, because of its ambiguity or due to an unfortunate choice of words. Or, I put myself into the patient's position and reflect upon my own last comment. Frequently this will alert me to the unintentional, and unconscious, communications that a patient could read into what I have just said. Then, when I listen to the patient's subsequent response, it becomes easier to see when this has been actually provoked by me, by my timing or manner of interpreting.

I first learned to monitor the therapeutic interaction in this way by trial-identifying with the patient when following the clinical presentations of people whom I supervised. With practice it becomes possible to use these two viewpoints simultaneously, the patient's and one's own, rather like following the different voices in polyphonic music.

This capacity to be in two places at once, in the patient's shoes and in one's own simultaneously, can only be encompassed if therapists can develop a capacity to synthesize these apparently paradoxical ego states. It is here, I believe, that the processing function of the internal supervisor comes to the fore. It is more than self-analysis and it is more than self-supervision.

The internal supervisor and play

Winnicott pointed out that:

> '*psychotherapy is done in the overlap of the two play areas, that of the patient and that of the therapist.* If the therapist cannot play, then he is not suitable for the work. If the patient cannot play, then something needs to be done to enable the patient to become able to play, after which psychotherapy may begin. The reason why playing is essential is that it is in playing that the patient is being creative.'
>
> (Winnicott 1971:54)

I regard playing as one of the functions of the internal supervisor, and it is through this that the therapist can share in the patient's creativity. It is also here that he can discover a balance between what he knows of the nature of the unconscious and the pitfalls of premature assumption.

Resisting pre-conceptions: an analogy from geometry

I wish to give an example of imaginative play in relation to psychotherapy. I also want to illustrate how there can be several different versions of 'original' image (or meaning) referred to, when we recognize that unconscious derivative communication frequently employs defensive forms of reference such as splitting and projection, displacement and reversal, etc. Here, I wish to illustrate some of these processes by using an imaginary shape from geometry.

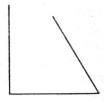

Figure 2

Suppose, for instance, that we are trying to make sense of a shape suggested by three lines of equal length (*Figure 2*). Let us also suppose that the three lines are joined, with two forming an angle of 60 degrees and the other line forming a right angle. If we are predisposed to find a triangle, we might regard the key to this shape as conveyed by the two lines at 60 degrees. The line at 90 degrees could then be regarded as out of place. If we play with this, as we might with a dream image (*Figure 3*), we could think of the 90 degrees angle as displaced – perhaps suggesting a defensive need not to represent the shape of a triangle in its un-disguised form. Prompted by that explanation, we could begin to think that we are 'really' being presented with a derivative representation of an equilateral triangle.

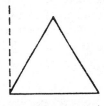

Figure 3

With the analytical predisposition to look for Oedipal material, it would be easy to formulate some triangular interpretation, regarding the 'dis-covered' triangle as having been defensively represented. We could think of the original shape as derived from a hidden triangle, being indirectly rather than directly alluded to.

If however we take another look at our imaginary shape we could orientate ourselves instead around the right-angle, and see the 60 degrees angle as a displacement – perhaps from another right angle (*Figure 4*). We might be looking at a derivative from a square, with one side unstated. Or we could be looking at a square-shaped 'U' or a 'container'; or (upside down) it could be a 'cover', that is if we do not confine ourselves only to the world of geometry.

It is this capacity for playing with a patient's images that Bion encouraged when he spoke of the analyst's use of 'reverie' (Bion 1967b:Chapter 9). He also gave a graphic illustration of this in his last paper to the British Psycho-

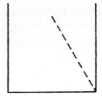

Figure 4

Analytical Society (1979, unpublished). He showed us how he arrived at a patient's particular question 'Why?' in the context of a patient's dream, in which the dreamer was being looked down upon by a crowd of people who were on a staircase that divided into the shape of a 'Y'.

Unfocused listening

Before giving an example of using internal supervision I wish to introduce the notion of 'unfocused listening'. I regard this as a first step beyond that of the familiar 'evenly suspended attention', with which analysts are encouraged to listen to the over-all drift of a patient's communications.

When I think that I am beginning to understand what is being communicated in a session, I find that it helps me to avoid pre-conceived ideas about this if I first abstract the recognizable themes from what a patient is saying, and hold these provisionally away from the overt context. Also, if I sometimes listen to the identified themes with unconscious symmetry in mind, it helps to show up the different possible meanings that can then emerge.

For instance, if a patient were to say 'My boss is angry with me', this can be silently abstracted as 'someone is angry with someone'. *Whose anger with whom* then remains unclear, and this can be considered with a more open mind than otherwise would be possible. It could be a statement of fact, objectively reported; it could be a reference to the patient's anger, projected onto the boss; it could be a displaced reference to the transference, the therapist seen as angry; or it could be an oblique reference to the patient being angry with the therapist. In practice, this balancing of different potential meanings needs to be integrated into the normal process of internal supervision.

The internal supervisor at work: an exercise in application

I shall now use a clinical vignette as an 'exercise', because we can more readily learn to recognize the various clinical options when we are not subjected to the pressures that exist in an actual therapy session. However, this is not intended as a model for conscious and active monitoring, or for choosing an interpretation in the session; nor should it be allowed to interfere with the therapist's 'free floating attention' during the session.

In order that we can develop a more subliminal use of the internal supervisor when we are with a patient, it is valuable to use (or, in a Winnicott sense, to 'play' with) clinical material outside of the session. A musician plays scales, or technical studies, in order that these can become a natural part of his technique. So too in psychotherapy: when a therapist is 'making music' with a patient he should not be preoccupied with issues of technique. That technique can be developed by taking time, away from the consulting room, for practising with clinical material. Then, when in the presence of a patient, the process of internal supervision is more readily available when it is most needed.

Example 2.1

A widow (Mrs J.) in her early forties comes to a session with these opening statements to her male therapist:

Patient: 'I have been wondering whether to go to a clairvoyant. (Pause.) I found a book of John's on his bookshelf, called *Father and Son*. I remember him talking about it as having been important to him, but I don't recall now what he said. I once started it, but I never really got into it. I suppose one day I ought to finish it.' (Pause.) 'I like reading, particularly Proust. It was John who first put me in touch with that. I'm glad he did. I began reading it again recently. That should fill a good many hours anyway.' (Pause.)

'I had a dream: *I saw a girl who was in difficulty in a fast running river. I thought she might be drowning, and wondered whether I should dive in to help her to get to safety.* I woke up before I did anything about it.' (Pause.) 'I wonder whether it is true that you see all of your life again when you are about to drown. I wouldn't have thought that there would be time. But the mind is very strange. Perhaps we will never know whether we can see our lives that clearly unless we are actually drowning.'

Passive recall

I have deliberately not given any background to this session, as I want to illustrate the usefulness of allowing the material of a session to evoke particular memories from earlier work with the patient. This helps a therapist not to enter a session laden with pre-conceived ideas, gained from earlier sessions. The paradox, of course, is that we do need to have an overview of the progression of any psychotherapy, while at the same time being able to leave that on one side to be recalled as needed.

We are here reminded that Mrs J.'s husband (John) died less than a year ago; and we need to know (from an earlier session) that Mrs J. had recently decided to buy a house away from London. She had given as her reasons for this that she wanted to get away from the constant reminders of John, in the house in which they had lived since they married; and she wanted her son (her only child) to go to the secondary school near where she had chosen to live. He was to start there after the summer holiday.

Mrs J.'s decision to move away from London had arisen suddenly, after only six months' therapy. We could therefore wonder whether she was afraid of getting into her deeper feelings, and whether this move might include an element of flight into health. (Her stated reasons were clearly important to her, so the therapist had resisted interpreting her move in case she took it as an attempt to control her decision about this.)

At this point in the therapy there were only five weeks until the therapist's summer holiday, and Mrs J. was planning to stop her sessions then. This ending felt abrupt and premature, but it was not until after this session that there was any open thinking about her other options.

Abstracting the themes

As we 'play' with this clinical material, using unfocused listening, we can note that there are several themes that are recurring. The clairvoyant suggests a wish to know about the future. If, however, we apply the concept of unconscious symmetry here we may be alerted to a possible primary-process equivalence of past and future. The unconscious theme therefore could be to do with a wish to make contact with *someone who is difficult to reach*, or *someone unreachable* (in the past or the future). We do not know whether this primarily refers to the husband, to the therapist representing the husband, or to the therapy. The clairvoyant could also be an unconscious metaphor for the patient's wish to have an alternative therapist, either because of the imminent end of therapy or because the patient may have experienced the therapist as not fore-seeing enough.

There are several details around the theme of *something unfinished*. For instance, there is the book that has been only partly read. This could refer equally to the unfinished relationship to the husband, or to the therapy that Mrs J. has only partly got into, or both. We can note too that, in the dream, Mrs J. begins to feel that she should dive in to rescue the drowning girl; but she wakes before she acts upon this. The death of her husband leaves much else that is unfinished, the marriage relationship and John's relationship with their son; and there is the title of the book which may be a further unconscious clue.

There is also a clear implication of *lost time*, in Mrs J.'s reference to Proust's *À la recherche du temps perdu*. The time lost most obviously refers to the cut-short marriage, but it could again prompt us to think of the therapy which is about to be cut short. Perhaps she has not had enough time to deal with the painful experiences that she has been through. Mrs J. points out she has a kind of self-therapy in mind; reading

Proust will fill many hours. There is a wish to recover time lost, to go over the past again, perhaps to keep memories alive. Mrs J. may be thinking about how else one can recall one's life. Does she have to be near to drowning to find out? This could be another reference to her wondering whether there would be time enough for that, perhaps also alluding to the planned ending of her therapy.

We might think of the father/son relationship. If we apply symmetry to this too, we are hearing about a *parent/child relationship*. Does this only refer to her son and his dead father? Could it also refer to herself as a child, and her father? (Her own father had died of a heart attack when she was twelve.) She may well be identifying with her son and his experience. They had both lost a father, at a similar age and in a similar way. We can wonder about the transference. Is the therapist representing her father here, who is about to be lost to Mrs J. before she is ready? The pattern of loss is apparent in all three sectors of her life, as if there were some unstoppable repetition operating. We can see this in her childhood, in her marriage, and now in her therapy – as it might seem to her.

Is this premature ending of therapy really so unstoppable? Has the therapist been going along with this as inevitable? Mrs J. could in fact get to London quite easily. It is only an hour away from her new home. Perhaps the therapist is referred to in the dream, as the person hesitating to rescue someone who is drowning.

Choice of interpretation: some examples

There are of course many possible responses to this material. Part of the work of internal supervision is to assess which could best serve the interests of the patient and of the therapeutic process. I shall give different possibilities, enlarging upon the options that might flash through my mind if I were to allow myself a 'period of hesitation' (Winnicott 1958:Chapter 4) before intervening.

Therapists need time to reflect, but the human mind can also work very quickly (like that of a drowning person) as long as the therapist is not himself feeling drowned by the quantity (or impact) of what a patient is saying. If he is feeling overwhelmed, it is often more useful to listen first to the *form* of the communication (its sheer weight or volume) before he risks getting lost in the detailed *content*.

Relating details to the therapy

A fairly common kind of interpretation here would be to play back the detail of the patient's communication, relating this to the therapy. But, when this is too all-embracing, it becomes like a lecture not an interpretation. For instance I have heard some responses to a patient that went something like:

> 'I think you would like me to be a clairvoyant, so that I could lessen your anxiety by knowing how things will be for you in the future. Also, as with the book that you have only begun to read, you may be wondering what is being left 'unread' by leaving your therapy early. We now do not have time to look more thoroughly at your past life, or your future; so it may be that in your dream you could be the drowning person, which suggests that I am represented as the person who is hesitating to dive in to rescue you. Instead of having further therapy you plan to read Proust to yourself, which could be your attempt to be a therapist to yourself, recovering what you can of your past life and doing this on your own.'

This covers most of what the patient has said, and brings it quite neatly together around the therapy. It may even be that it is all correct. Internal supervision, however, would help us to recognize that it lacks focus. This becomes even clearer if we use trial identification. What could a patient's response be to this? Suppose she were to say 'Yes' to this long interpretation, what would she be saying 'Yes' to?

We might also pick up a sense of the patient being bombarded by such an all-embracing interpretation. The patient could either be impressed by the skill of the therapist, in being able to fit everything together like this (if it did fit), or she could feel irritated by the basic assumption that everything is being related to the therapist as if it were bound to be so.

This style of interpretation is unlikely to enhance the therapeutic process. It leaves no room for the patient to offer leads of her own, towards distinguishing which part of what she has communicated is most urgent to her at this point in the session.

A *full transference interpretation*

What I am here calling a *full* transference interpretation is that in which it is possible to bring together the three elements that are usually linked in a dynamically complete interpretation of transference: (a) the patient's present life; (b) the therapeutic relationship; (c) the patient's past. (NB It is often forgotten that it may take several sessions, or even weeks, before a full transference interpretation can be convincingly offered to a patient, whether based on a dream or other communications.)

A transference interpretation here could be formed by linking together the following elements in the patient's current experience: in her present life (the ongoing impact of her husband's death); in her childhood (the death of her father); and in the therapeutic relationship (the impending end). We could therefore interpret:

> 'You are concerned with a repeating pattern of premature endings: the death of your husband, and in your childhood of your father, and now I may have come to represent husband *and* father as we approach the ending of your therapy.'

Many therapists would accept this kind of interpretation as applicable, and perhaps as necessary, here. It is more focused than the previous example, because it draws upon a fuller abstracting of the themes, and it offers a single integration of these around the focus upon premature endings.

Our internal supervision, however, should point out the predictability of such an interpretation. It is almost a standard comment, and patients who have had regular interpretations of this kind expect the therapist to do exactly this again, with almost whatever they say. Trial-identifying with the patient can prompt us to recognize when a patient could reply: 'I thought you might say that.' This is not proof of the accuracy of an interpretation so much as of the expectability of it. And therapists do not need to tell patients what they already know.

In this session, it is possible that the patient might be able to use this particular transference interpretation because it has impact. The fact that the therapy does not have to end could emerge out of this. Equally, the patient might recognize, perhaps for the first time, the extent to which the death of her husband has come to be re-enacted within the therapy even to the extent of the patient setting up a premature ending of the treatment.

My main reservation, in this instance, would be to do with the timing. It would carry more conviction, if the therapist were to wait until it becomes clearer that the patient is needing this kind of interpretation. Here it could appear to be arrived at more by rule of thumb.

The deepest anxiety

Another possible interpretation, aimed at the patient's deepest anxiety in this sequence, could be to pick out the unconscious implications of the dream. (We need to know that Mrs J. had repeatedly been angry with the hospital and the doctors, that they had not done more to save her husband's life.)

It is possible to see a reference in the dream to some life-saving action that is withheld. We could wonder about Mrs J.'s earlier signs of projected guilt, in blaming others. (The therapist had previously heard her pleading that she had not realized that a mild heart attack could be so quickly and fatally repeated. She had thought that her husband had recovered more than he had. She had been relieved when they had been able to resume a normal life, after he had recovered from his first heart attack.)

We could wonder about Mrs J.'s unconscious guilt, and her possible collusion with her husband's resumed level of normal activity. Had she been blaming herself for not having taken the risk to his life more seriously? Does the drowning girl (in the dream) represent her husband whose life had been at risk? Does the dream represent her husband as a girl because the undisguised truth here could have been too painful to the patient? If we think this to be so, and if we believe that the patient needs to face this pain along with her unconscious guilt, we could say:

> 'I think that you are blaming yourself for what you see as your part in your husband's death, as if you feel there might have been something you could have done to have saved him from this. So, in the dream, there is a person that you recognize as drowning but you wake up to reality before you have acted upon this.'

Here there is a technical problem. If a therapist prematurely interprets some assumed unconscious guilt, he can be experienced by the patient as suggesting that she should feel guilty. If he claims to see evidence of unconscious guilt, or the assumed cause of such guilt, before the patient begins to be aware of this, that assumption of the therapist can no longer be regarded merely as the patient's projection or transference.

By using trial identification, we can assess more sensitively whether this patient is actually indicating a readiness for an exploration of possible unconscious guilt; or might this focus for interpretation merely induce guilt without leaving time, in this session or even in the remaining therapy, for it to be worked through? Our listening to that possible intervention, from the position of the patient, might prompt us to remain cautious and not yet to offer any interpretation aimed at her supposed unconscious guilt.

Finding a bridge to an interpretation

It is important that therapists should find ways to interpret to patients, which do not interfere with the drift of their own emerging thoughts. It is also important that they do not pre-empt a patient's experience, by interrupting what he or she is beginning to feel, or by anticipating what is not yet being felt by the patient. It will often be the case, therefore, that therapists do not have sufficient evidence for any interpretation as such. This does not mean that they ask questions to elicit the evidence they lack. Equally it does not always mean that they just remain in silence until further information emerges. Sometimes a patient is better able to continue if a therapist simply indicates that he has been following.

So, instead of interpreting, there are occasions when a

therapist has to look for an intermediate step that brings to a manageable focus what has been said so far. This should maintain as fully as possible the patient's freedom to continue in any direction, rather than in a direction indicated by comments from the therapist.

Here, for instance, we cannot assume that the reference to drowning necessarily relates to the therapy more than to anything else. If the therapist had forgotten, or did not know, that this patient was currently approaching the anniversary of her husband's death, it would be a hurtful assumption to presume that her distress was to do mainly with her therapist. It might therefore be preferable, at this point in the session, not to assume any reference to the therapist even if it might be around. Instead we could look for a more neutral way of playing back the themes to her.

We can note the theme of things that are unfinished. We can also recognize a sense of urgency in the dream. We could therefore show that we are aware of this by saying something like:

> 'Running through what you have told me, I notice that there are several references to things left unfinished; and there is also a sense of urgency in the dream about a person who might be drowning.'

From a neutral playback such as this, the patient could lead on to the issue of whether or not to end her therapy; or she could surprise us by leading straight into the anniversary mourning. This may, or may not, subsequently come to be linked to the proposed ending of her therapy. If it is not, we might again feel it to be important that we offer a way of leaving the patient to find this for herself, preferably without her being directed to it. A further bridge comment, which might serve that purpose, could be:

> 'One question, that you may be asking yourself in your dream, is whether all endings have to be unstoppable and final. There is a fast-flowing river which cannot be stopped, but it may be possible to rescue the girl from drowning.'

The most urgent anxiety

One way of focusing an interpretation here would be around
the sense of urgency, which is clearly indicated in the dream.
Some action is called for, to save someone from drowning.
The most immediate context for this dream is likely to be the
fact that the time for therapy is running out.

If we feel that the patient is needing to recognize the
self-destructiveness in her premature ending of therapy, and
there is not much time left to deal with this, we might say to the
patient:

> 'I think you are anxious about the approaching end of
> your therapy. Time is running out, as things stand, and
> you may be wondering whether I will do anything to
> prevent what (in your dream) is represented as a
> drowning.'

Our trial identification here might still prompt us to pause
before offering this interpretation. The patient may be
waiting for the therapist to stop her leaving. If he were to act
upon this wish she could experience this as manipulative –
even as a seductive move by him. She might get to this on her
own, from a half-interpretation as described in the preceding
section (pp. 46-7).

The therapist would have to balance the possible gains or
losses for this patient. If he does not pre-empt her recognition
of the need for her therapy to continue, she might arrive at
this for herself and could accept any decision to continue
therapy more clearly as her own. On the other hand, if the
patient's self-destructiveness is being denied, it would amount
to a collusion if the therapist were to sit back passively without
challenging her. He would have to assess the patient's readiness to recognize the self-destructiveness for herself, or her
degree of unconscious resistance to seeing this, before decid-
ing upon whether to confront her. Depending upon the
particular patient, quite different courses here might be
preferred.

I have offered five contrasting ways of responding to this
material, and of course there are others. No therapist could

consciously explore so many options (even silently) within an on-going session unless a patient happens to allow time for this. Nevertheless, some of this reflection might be fleetingly noted, even if only at a preconscious level. It is always important that therapists learn to recognize alternative ways in which they might respond.

I have given a sample of what I am calling 'playing scales' with clinical material, in order to illustrate some of the technical issues. If a therapist does not rush in to intepret, internal supervision can more easily process the options that are available and the implications of each.

From supervisor to internal supervision

The shift from an initial dependence upon the external supervisor, via the internalized supervisor, to a more autonomous internal supervision is a slow process – and at times it will not be steady. To illustrate some stages in this development I will give a brief clinical example of each.

Internal supervision being absent

Example 2.2

A patient was being seen in therapy three times a week with a male therapist. She spent the first half of a session swamping her therapist with details of depression, promiscuous sexuality, scenes of violence, etc. There was a general feeling of no containment or control anywhere.

The therapist stayed silent, unable to find any meaningful way into the session. The patient then left the session to go to the toilet, which she always did at least once in every session. Upon returning, she closed the consulting room door and appeared to change the subject.

Comment: The therapist might have been able to find release from his sense of paralysis if he had commented on the form of this patient's communication, her pouring out of details and her need to relieve herself of anxiety (in the toilet), as indicating her fear that her therapist could not offer the relief or the containment she was so urgently in search of.

The session continued as follows:

> *Patient:* 'I cannot sleep unless I have the windows and doors all tight shut.'
> *Therapist:* 'Was your mother like that?'
> *Patient:* 'Yes...' (Lots of details followed.)

Comment: Important opportunities for following the patient can be lost when a therapist diverts the session by introducing a new focus of attention. So, when a therapist points the patient to the past (as in a transference interpretation), it is as well to check whether he or she could be taking refuge from stress in the session by a defensive manoeuvre of flight to the past.

Discussion: Upon presenting this material in supervision, the therapist had initially been pleased with the wealth of new detail from his patient's childhood, which followed from this single question. After all, therapists are told that one indication of an effective interpretation is that new material emerges from the patient. If, however, we follow this sequence from an interactional viewpoint, suspending our trial identification equally between therapist and patient, we arrive at a quite different formulation of this exchange.

Before the therapist's first intervention we can see that the patient's behaviour in the session was similar to her life outside. She was pouring out detail, as discharge rather than as a communication, and the themes were of non-containment, both sexual and aggressive. My trial identification with the therapist here highlights the pressure he is under from the patient. The patient then leaves the session, to get rid of her discomfort into the toilet. This is further discharge of unease through action. There is no containment.

Upon resuming her session, the patient's first communication (non-verbal and verbal) had to do with doors and windows. These could be symbols for the containment she is needing. She points out that, for her, they have to be firmly closed if she is to feel secure. However, the therapist thinks that he is being given a cue to explore this 'symptomatic behaviour' in terms of the patient's childhood so he asks about the patient's mother.

If we again listen to this interactionally, we can sense the therapist's unconscious communication to the patient. There are a number of qualities to this particular question. It puts a pressure on the patient to answer it. (Is the therapist feeling under pressure; and he is reversing this onto the patient, i.e. unconsciously retaliating?) It deflects the patient from the present to the past. (Is the therapist needing a breather from what had been around in the session up until then?) It deflects the patient away from the therapist onto the patient's mother. (Is there something that is uncomfortable for the therapist to stay with, in the therapeutic relationship?) These are all possible reasons for him resorting here to a deflection of the focus in the session.

When the patient follows the unconscious lead given to her by the therapist, she may be joining him in a shared search for relief from something that *both* could have been finding difficult to cope with in the present. If the therapist were using his own trial identification he might have been prompted to re-assess this sequence. The patient is reponding to a deflective lead provided by the therapist.

The willing production of new detail here therefore does not indicate an intuitively apt question. It could instead be evidence of a shared defense, the therapist and patient together moving off to past history where feelings are more distant and where the details discussed do not refer specifically *either* to the patient *or* to the therapist. Talking about the mother's pathology can become a collusive avoidance of the present, and of the relationship between the patient and therapist — not all of which is transference. It will also be noticed by the patient that this avoidance of the present has been instigated by the therapist, with the result that what had been difficult for the patient to contain could be seen as uncontainable by therapist and patient alike.

Using the internalized supervisor

Example 2.3

A therapist seeing a male patient, early in therapy, found

herself being over-active in several sessions. This seemed to be in response to a characteristic passivity with which this patient had approached life, including the question of referral for therapy.

In the session immediately prior to the therapist coming for supervision, the following interchange took place:

> *Patient:* 'I can't remember where we left off at the end of the last session.'
> *Therapist:* 'Perhaps if you let your mind wander you will be able to remember.'

During the supervision I had said that this reply could confirm the patient's impression that he should try to link one session with the other. The notion of staying with the present, whatever that may lead to, is not yet clear to this patient.

The next session began as follows:

> *Patient:* 'I am trying to let my mind wander, to see if that helps me to remember the last session. I'm not sure that it's going to work for me.'
> *Therapist:* 'I may have given you a misleading impression in what I said last time. What I meant to say was that it doesn't matter in therapy whether one session clearly links up with the previous one, or not. You can start anywhere, and we can see where it goes.'
> *Patient:* 'Well, I am now thinking about learning to swim with my older sister helping me. She knew just when to hold me and when to let go, so that I could begin to swim on my own. The same happened when I was learning to ride a bicycle. She started by holding the steering wheel for me, and the saddle. She later just held the saddle while I steered; and then she began to let go until I was riding on my own.'

Discussion: This patient responded immediately with memories that related to the need to shift from someone steering or holding him (both being forms of controlling) to letting go — so that he could be free to use the psychotherapeutic process more autonomously and actively than had been happening hitherto.

This example illustrates a therapist drawing upon her previous supervision (using the 'internalized supervisor'). In recognizing and responding to the patient's cue, in this next session, she also shows that she is beginning to develop and to use her own internal supervision.

Using internal supervision

In order to point to the use of internal supervision in settings other than just therapy and analysis, I include here a vignette from my own earlier experience as a social worker.

Example 2.4

Teddy, as his mother called him, was twenty-four when I first met him. For two years he had been treated at home, on stelazine, as a catatonic schizophrenic. He had formerly been treated in a mental hospital until his mother insisted on having him back home.

Teddy's mother asked me to see him because she felt it might be possible to begin getting through to him; he had started to give single-word answers to questions. I agreed to see him once a week. His mother began to bring him to my office, leading him by the hand, and she would then wait downstairs until he was ready to go home. It was as if he were a toddler being taken to play-school.

During the first few weeks I was able to get three different one-word responses from Teddy: 'Yes', 'No' and 'not really'. From these answers, and by asking specific leading questions, I was able to gather from him that he had a brother four years younger than himself. I was also able to get some details about his home and school, and the fact that he had had a job for two years after leaving school. For some reason that was unclear he had been dismissed from that job, since when he had remained permanently not speaking.

Internal supervision: **Although it could be thought that I was making progress with Teddy, by getting these details out of him, I became very uneasy about the nature of the interaction between myself and him. Nothing seemed to be achieved during my attempts at using silence with him: nothing other than factual information was being gained through this active questioning.**

I imagined myself in his place, wondering what it might be like having a social worker intermittently firing questions at me like that. It soon struck me how persecutory that could be. It was as if I were trying to force myself through Teddy's near total exclusion of the outside world: and his mode of answering seemed to be a compromise between his need to defend himself from intrusion and the pressures (from me) for him to speak. I resolved to try a different approach.

When Teddy next came to my office I had moved our chairs from their previous position (almost face to face) to being more nearly parallel. When we were seated I began to speak – half to Teddy and half to myself.

Social worker: 'I have arranged the chairs differently today for a reason that I will try to explain. I have been thinking how it might feel being *you* here, with a social worker who has been firing all these questions at you. I have also wondered if it might be easier for us both if I didn't sit so directly opposite you – looking as if I am expecting you to look back at me.' (Silence.)

'When I imagine being in your place, with all those questions coming at me, I feel as if someone we're trying to get inside me – forcing me to give away bits of myself that I might not want to give away.' (Silence.) 'I have an image of being surrounded by people trying to force me to talk, and wanting to hide from them. I can also imagine myself not talking to anyone, as a way of trying to build a wall around me to keep people out.' (Pause.)

'Unfortunately, until today, I have been failing to recognize that you might be needing to keep up a wall of silence as a way of keeping me out and at a safe distance.' (Teddy turned his head towards me with a look of interest.)

Teddy: 'It's funny you put it like that. I have often thought of myself as hiding under a man-hole cover, in a drain, with people trying to find me – and sewage down below. I'm not afraid of drains. It's people that smell. They make it difficult for me to breathe. My mother suffocates me. She treats me like a little boy. I am really a man inside, you know. She doesn't realize that.'

I was astonished. Teddy had been almost entirely silent for over two years. The only exceptions had been his single-word answers, with which he had parried questions from those around him. Now, quite unexpectedly, he was beginning to express his own thoughts and feelings.

Discussion: By putting myself in his place, I had come to recognize Teddy's need for his defensive withdrawal. Only when I stopped being an 'impinging object' could he begin to feel free to reach out to me – as someone he could begin to relate to. In particular, I had to be aware of his need for space and separateness in a world that had become persistently intrusive. Like other people, I had originally responded to his silence by also becoming intrusive. It was only by using trial identification, to monitor his experience of me, that I became aware of the nature of this interaction.

We still had far to go beyond this beginning, but it was a start that Teddy was able to build upon. After six months he persuaded his mother to desist from bringing him. Thereafter he always came on his own, and he began to use his sessions spontaneously without any leading from me. In the second year he found himself a job in a toy shop. There he could relate to parents and children on his own terms.

In the rest of this book I shall give other illustrations of internal supervision being used clinically, or missing. I hope also to show how this process needs to settle into a background level of functioning. Too active a preoccupation of self-monitoring can disturb the free-floating attention (see Chapter Five). But, there are many times too when the analytic work can be rescued from foundering by learning to sense how a patient could be experiencing the therapist, in the kind of ways that I have been describing.

Notes

1. In the paper referred to (originally presented to social workers) I suggest that, when there are two people working together with a family or marital couple, it is important to establish a 'supervisory viewpoint' to which each worker can refer in thinking about what is happening in the interview or session. From this viewpoint, the social workers concerned can examine the interaction between them for ways in which this may be reflecting unconscious aspects of the family or marital interaction. The clinical value of this later prompted me to consider using a similar reference point, within the single worker or therapist, which I now call the 'internal supervisor'. (I outline this paper here as it is likely, by now, to be out of print.)

2. It may help the reader to know that all the extended clinical presentations in this book (Chapters Three, Five, Seven and Nine) were written before my thinking in this present chapter had been formulated. In fact it was that work, with those earlier patients, which prompted me to examine more closely the processes upon which I have in particular focused in this chapter.

3. I outline what I mean by an interactional viewpoint in the next chapter.

3

Internal supervision: a lapse and recovery

In this chapter I wish to show how patients respond to a therapist's errors. The example I shall give is of a time when I failed to remain in a professional role. We will see how the patient gives unconscious prompts towards a recovery of the therapy when this is in danger of collapse.

I shall also use this clinical sequence to demonstrate the different clinical perspectives that are opened up when one examines the therapeutic relationship from a viewpoint that takes into account the unconscious interaction between patient and therapist, in which each is responding to cues from the other.

An interactional viewpoint outlined

Since the papers on countertransference by Heimann (1950) and Little (1951), it has been increasingly recognized that the analytic relationship is one in which there are two people interacting. Each is seeking to get to know the other. Consciously or unconsciously each is affecting the other. This dimension to the analytic relationship is implicit (and sometimes explicit) throughout the writings of such authors as Balint, Winnicott, Bion, Sandler and Searles, to name just a few. Langs, on the other hand, has made an extensive study of these phenomena.[1]

It is no longer adequate to think of the analyst as the one who observes and interprets, and the patient as the only person in this relationship who presents evidence of unconscious communications and pathology. Patients do not see the analyst as a blank screen. They scrutinize the analyst, who aims to remain inscrutable, and they find many clues to the nature of this person they are dealing with. They sense the state of mind of the analyst and respond accordingly.

Analysts and therapists often give away more about themselves than they realize. They might not speak openly about themselves, and they can be careful about personal questions, but they do not remain a closed book to the patient. Like a child who watches the mother's face for signs of pleasure or indications of mood, patients listen for similar signs from the therapist and there are many available.

Patients monitor changes in the manner of the therapist's presence, for instance his state of relaxation or his fidgeting in sessions. They also note the unconscious implications indicated by the nature of his comments. These interventions are not always interpretive – making conscious what is emerging from the patient's unconscious. They may be directive, suggesting what the patient should do or feel; or intrusive, as with questions; or they may be deflective, inviting a change of focus, which can suggest that the therapist is avoiding something difficult in the session.

Patients notice the selection and timing of the therapist's interventions. They ask themselves why this is commented on and not that, and why the therapist intervenes when he does, rather than sooner or later (or not at all). Patients also pick up the therapist's anxiety when he is over-active or interruptive in a session. Likewise they wonder about prolonged silences, particularly when a flood of the patient's strong feelings has been expressed. Has the therapist been overwhelmed by the patient?

At least unconsciously, and sometimes consciously, patients will be interpreting the therapist to themselves. They even offer unconscious interpretations to the therapist (Little 1951:381). When the therapist is seen as defensive he is also seen as feeling threatened. This raises anxiety about his capacity to contain the patient. One response is for the patient to behave protectively towards the therapist, by displacing more difficult feelings onto others, or introjectively against themselves. A patient's more hopeful response challenges the therapist's defensiveness, drawing his attention to whatever appears to be amiss. Patients always note the degree to which a therapist is ready to stay in touch with what is being communicated. So, it is important that therapists recognize elements of objective reality in the consulting room to which a patient could be responding. It is here in particular that trial identification offers valuable insight to the therapist.

Whenever I say something in therapy, or continue to say nothing, I am having an effect upon the patient. I therefore need to listen for the patient's responses to my input, some of which initially may be beyond my immediate consciousness. Listening to myself in the place of the patient can help to bring the dynamics of this interaction more into the field of my awareness.

Frequently, patients show a double response to a therapist's contribution to a session. At one level they respond to the external reality; at another they elaborate on it in terms of past experience and their inner reality. So, even when a patient's responses can be considered as transference, these are often initiated by external triggers in the session from the therapist (see Chapter Five).

It follows that I often cannot understand what a patient is trying to communicate to me until I can identify the nature of my own contributions in a session to which a patient may be responding. When I can identify the trigger(s) to a patient's responses I am able to understand the patient differently and (I believe) more pertinently. Therefore, like a blind man, I try to listen for the different kinds of echo that are reflected back to me from each step that I take in a session. This is how I think of an interactional viewpoint to listening. It helps me to be in touch with my own effects upon a patient as distinct from what arises more autonomously from within the patient. I also try to monitor the patient's effects upon me.

The use of an interactional viewpoint is implicit throughout this book. I outline it here because I give specific examples in this chapter, and in Chapter Five, of my own early attempts at using this way of listening to patients. I shall look more extensively at the nature of patients' unconscious cues and prompts in Chapter Eight.

Introduction to the clinical presentation

The clinical work I use to illustrate the theme of this chapter was undertaken at a time when I had not yet worked out my thoughts as in Chapter Two; so I had not established internal supervision as a regular process in my listening. Previously, I had used this mainly when I knew that I was under stress, or when the patient was in crisis; I still had to learn that there is an additional need for self-monitoring at times when the therapy seems to be going well. What follows, therefore, are two occasions of countertransference folly.

Whenever a therapist acts upon his countertransference, there is a need for self-analysis to understand what has been happening and why. There is also a need to attend to the disruptive effects of this upon the therapy. here an inter-actional view to listening turns out to be particularly helpful, the more so as I was not being supervised on this case at the time reported. We will see how the patient indicates the various levels at which she was responding to my stepping out of role. She also demonstrates how perceptively she had been follow-ing my part in her sessions.

Had I remained unaware of acting out my countertransfer-ence, my intrusive behaviour could have brought this therapy to an abrupt and destructive close. Fortunately, I was able to recover from this lapse through recognizing the patient's unconscious prompts. I could easily have missed the signi-ficance of these cues, if I had not already become aware of the ways in which patients can reflect their valid perceptions of the therapist's unconscious (Langs 1978).

Background to session[2]

Mrs A. was in her sixties when she entered once-a-week therapy. She was referred for severe anxiety attacks with a history of manic-depressive mood swings. Initially, therapy had failed to contain the patient, and she was hospitalized. Lithium Carbonate therapy was begun by the psychiatrist, who took over the treatment. Later, at the request of Mrs A., I was asked to resume her psychotherapy while she was still in hospital. This began to be more meaningful to her and she was discharged from the hospital. Not long afterwards, her wish for the medication to be discontinued was also agreed to.

Mrs A. began to make significant progress in many areas of her life. The anxiety attacks ceased over a period of two years, and there was no re-occurrence of the earlier uncontrollable mood swings. The patient was pleased with her progress and so was I. This situation, however, led to a more relaxed relationship, with me 'soft-pedalling' during a period that seemed to be a prelude to ending therapy. At the time, I rationalized this shift towards a more realistic and mutual relationship in terms of my residual belief that it might enable the transference relationship to be worked through and relinquished more easily. I no longer believe that. It was a left-over from my earlier work, as social worker and as inexperienced therapist.

What I did not know at this time was that the patient was approaching a crisis in her marriage. Stresses had been developing at home because her husband had relied upon his wife's readiness to avoid conflict by her dutiful compliance to his wishes and demands. During therapy Mrs A. had discovered that she could stand up for herself with her husband, even if doing so led to conflict, but this growth in her was creating pressures for change in the marriage. There had been hints of this problem in the past, but a more direct presentation of these marital difficulties was postponed until I had attended to the period of professional laxity here described.

Recent breaks in the therapeutic frame[3]

About two months prior to the session to be quoted, Mrs A. had been praising her dentist (Dr X.). Even though it meant travelling a long distance to see him, she had been treated by this same man for years, as he had always been careful and thorough in his work. Recently she had been able to combine her weekly visits for therapy with going to this dentist, whose surgery was just down the road from my consulting rooms.

Here I fell into a countertransference gratification as a result of my own need for a good dentist. I felt tantalized by the patient's unsolicited testimonial of her dentist, and asked her if she would mind giving me his name as I was looking for a reliable dentist for myself. Mrs A. readily gave this and said she was glad to be of help. She hoped that I would find Dr X. as good as she always had.

Comment: We will see later a typical split between the patient's conscious pleasure at being able to be of help and her unconscious resentment at the implications of this request for *her* attention to *my* needs. We will also see how one exception often leads to another.

Two sessions before the one to be presented, I asked the patient for another favour. Mrs A. had been speaking of her occasional difficulty in getting to sleep, and of how useful she had found a relaxation tape to be. This tape was so effective for her that she had never yet heard it to the end it as she was always asleep by then.

I said I would be interested in hearing this tape. Mrs A. replied by saying that she could tell me where I could get it. She then correctly assessed that I was hinting at borrowing *her* tape. She said that perhaps I would prefer to hear it before making the commitment of buying a copy for myself. She offered to bring it with her the next week to lend to me. Her husband could make her a copy in case she needed to use it while I had the original.

Comment: My listening has veered completely away from the patient. As with the earlier reference to her good dentist, I am responding like an envious child. Each time Mrs A. indicates that she has something good, I have wanted some of it for myself and I have asked the patient to provide it for me. The patient is unlikely to miss the unconscious implications here concerning difficulties I might be having in managing something in myself. She may be wondering whether I am telling her that I too am having sleeping problems, as I seem to be asking her obliquely to help me with this. My countertransference gratification is clearly evident.

I thanked Mrs A. and accepted her offer. She brought the tape to her next session; and her last words in that session were: 'I don't know why, but to-day doesn't seem to have been as helpful as I had hoped.'

Comment: I have not yet responded to the patient's unconscious efforts to alert me to this role-reversal; and my accepting the loan of the tape, even after having had a week to reflect on the implications of this action, could confirm the patient's fear that I have not yet recognized my need to attend to something wrong in the therapy. It also demonstrates a continuing lack of alertness in my self-supervision. Her closing words express a sense of disappointment about the session. This time, however, I notice her unconscious prompt and I am able to make use of it in the following session.

The session

Mrs A. came in and sat down. I handed back the tape and thanked her for letting me listen to it. I made no further reference to this, not wanting to lead into a discussion about it, and neither did she. She put the tape on the table between us and left it there throughout the session.

Internal supervision: By leaving the tape on the table the patient could be indicating that this remains an issue to be attended to.

Mrs A. proceeded to show me a new Bible, which her husband had just given to her for a wedding anniversary present. Her husband knew that it was just what she wanted. I looked at it briefly and handed it back to her, saying that it was certainly a very beautiful Bible.

Internal supervision: I am still caught into the quasi-social relationship, which I had initiated earlier. The patient demonstrates a split response. She uses the same kind of break in the frame, handing something else to me for my approval. We may also speculate that Mrs A. has become concerned about my seductiveness, in my neglect of the usual professional boundaries, and this could be why she is symbolically bringing her husband in here. She may be reminding me that she is a married woman.

> Mrs A. said she had had a terrible week and could not think why. Nevertheless, she had been able to sleep every night except the last. She had been using her copy of the relaxation tape, made for her by her husband, but the previous night she had not used it because she was afraid she might not wake up in time and could miss her session.

Internal supervision: The patient may be rebuking me for having caused her to sleep badly. There could also be some wish to miss the session expressed in her anxiety about over-sleeping.

> Mrs A. said she could not remember what had happened during the last session. She went on to say that she had had a fall during the week. She had thought for a moment that there might have been something wrong with *her*, that she could have had a blackout; but she came to realize that this was not what had happened. She had tripped over a badly laid paving-stone: 'It was very uneven and dangerous. It really isn't safe leaving pavements in that condition. So many people fall over them, and some get seriously hurt, but the authorities always find ways to shelve the blame. They still don't do anything to put it right.'

Internal supervision: The patient may be commenting on my recent behaviour. Has she introjected my own tripping up? And has this come to be enacted in her falling, she wondering at first whether it might have been *her* fault? She later realized that it was not something wrong with herself, but was due to the unevenness of what she had been walking on. This feels like an unconscious reference to the unevenness of my work with her, and my failure to maintain a sufficiently secure basis for the therapy. The patient points out that this unevenness could be dangerous. The themes continue around blame being shelved and nothing being done about it. If this does refer unconsciously to the unevenness of my recent work, the patient may be expressing her fear that nothing will be done about putting things right.

> Mrs A. continued by saying that over the weekend she had suddenly developed a terrible abscess under the root of a front tooth, that resulted in the worst pain she had ever experienced. She had 'phoned Dr X. (the dentist), and he had told her to come right over. She went to see him that Monday. He had examined her carefully and said that she certainly had an abscess; but there was nothing wrong with her tooth, so she must be run down or something. She could not think why this should be so. True, she said, she had gone away to St. Mary's Rest Home recently, hoping to come away feeling much better, but she had left there feeling just the same.

(*Note*: As I recognized that it was an important session in this therapy, I made notes on the clinical sequence immediately afterwards. At this point they continue verbatim – as far as I could recall what was actually said. I quote direct from those notes.)

> *Patient:* 'I'll say this for Dr X., he did something they don't often seem to do nowadays. When there's poison there underneath I think it is better to lance it, or in some other way to help the poison to come out, and that is exactly what he did. He removed a filling, which allowed the abscess to drain out, and it feels much better now. He gave me penicillin too, which probably helps, but it always makes me feel terribly exhausted. Doctors often just give you a pill, or whatever, and expect that to deal with the problem without doing anything more about it.'

Internal supervision: The patient now speaks of work done thoroughly, where the root-cause of something wrong is radically and carefully dealt with. She compares this with other more casual ways of dealing with patients. Mrs A. reports having fallen, and then developing this abscess, but she continues to look for proper treatment. It is also worth noting that an earlier break in the frame, concerning the dentist, had been left unattended to and may be alluded to here.

Comment: If this contrast is thought of as referring to the therapy, it is not surprising that therapists are not always willing to recognize their work reflected by patients in ways like this.

> *Therapist:* 'I believe you are pointing out to me some of what has been wrong with your recent sessions. Last week you had come expecting that something troubling you would be properly attended to. You left feeling that the session had not been helpful.'

> *Patient:* 'I didn't think I was criticizing you in what I was saying, but I suppose it is possible that I was. I don't claim to be much good at understanding these things.'

Internal supervision: The patient is prepared to consider that she could be expressing criticism of me. She speaks of herself as not claiming to be much good at understanding these things. This may be a further introjective reference to me as a therapist who does claim to understand these things, but lately has been failing to do so.

> *Patient:* 'I've got some good news to tell you. Although John [her husband] and Anne [her daughter] are both being rather difficult still, James [her son] has been a great help. An old lady's electric kettle had not been working. She had taken it to the Electricity Board repair-desk, where she was told it needed a new heating element and this would cost £4 if someone else could fit it for her, or £10 if she left it at the desk.'

(*Note:* It so happened that the patient's fee was also £10 per session.)

The patient continued:

> 'The old lady could not afford to pay that, so she had offered it to Anne for her annual charity bring-and-buy sale. James

offered to look at the kettle, and shortly afterwards came back with it mended. He'd seen that the flex was all rotten, and needed renewing, and the plug was also cracked in two places. He'd replaced the flex and the plug, and the kettle was working perfectly. James now plans to see what other electrical things this old lady has that might have dangerous flexes or plugs, and he will be checking everything over for her. It could have been lethal. Fancy someone at the Electricity Board not seeing that this was wrong, and handing it back in that condition! They of all people should have known better. I suppose nowadays there are lots of people who don't do a proper job. They just sit back and take the money, and don't bother about the consequences.'

Internal supervision: The themes remain the same – jobs not done properly; faults are left that could be lethal – and there are references to more than a single fault being revealed upon proper inspection; and we hear of people (who should know better) failing to recognize what is wrong. It happens that there is more than one break in the usual boundaries to therapy, which were still needing to be dealt with. I also note this reference to money being taken for poor work. As this session is the last of the month, and the patient would be expecting to receive the monthly account, it is difficult not to feel that she is making some reference to me here – seeing me as recently having been sitting back in the therapy.

Therapist: 'You are giving me more examples of jobs not being done properly, because people do not bother to see what is wrong, compared with James taking the trouble to look into what was wrong and putting right those faults that could have been seriously dangerous or even lethal. I think you are still wondering whether I am bothering to do a proper job here, or am I just sitting back and taking the money without adequately dealing with what is wrong.'

Patient: 'Well, now that you come to point this out, I have been wondering about the way in which you work. For instance, it is like a machine; let's say a tape recorder (and she looks at the tape on the side-table), where something is wrong so that only some of what is being said is recorded. When you play it back, there are bits that are so faint you cannot hear it properly. Now, take something like my visits to St. Mary's. I know you know, at least I assume you know, that that is something important to me and yet you don't ask me about it. I might go on for a whole session to see if you will, but you don't. So when you don't, I'm not sure if you really care. On the other hand, I have assumed it must be because you want to leave me room to say what else may be on my mind. But you do sometimes ask. For instance, you always asked about my leg after my accident, and would offer me the footstool when I was having to keep my leg up as much as possible.'

Internal supervision: The patient has been following my way of working very closely, and has been trying to understand why I work in this way. In particular, she is trying to understand why I have been inconsistent. She indicates the tape as a part of what is wrong. She goes on from there to give an example of a listening machine that is not functioning properly. There is a strong impression that these may be derivative references to my lapses in attention, my recent failures to listen adequately. The patient goes on to wonder whether I care. In her example, she refers to a time when I had been functioning more appropriately, leaving her space to say what was on her mind; but she concludes with a further reference to my inconsistency. The offering of the footstool is also a move away from the formal therapeutic relationship, and is referred to along with the other exceptions.

> Therapist: 'I think that the key to this is that you have experienced a confusing degree of unevenness in the way I have been working with you. Part of you would like me to offer a more social kind of relationship; and when I do you may be consciously glad of that, as with the footstool. But you actually need me to remain a therapist in this relationship.' (Pause.)
>
> 'When I have been more clearly a therapist you have been

able to make sense of what I do, so long as I have been consistent. What has been confusing to you has been when I have shifted between being therapist at one moment and being more social with you at another, thereby entering into superficial exchanges with you that result in my not listening or attending adequately to the underlying problems. My borrowing of the tape is an example of this, and it has become a further source of confusion to you.'

Patient: 'I must admit I was very surprised when you said you would be interested in hearing that tape, but I thought it was nice to see you being human and to be of use to you. After all, you have been a great help to me in the past.'

Internal supervision: The patient feels free to acknowledge her surprise at my behaviour, now that I indicate I am prepared to look at this myself. She softens this, nevertheless, perhaps in order not to hurt me as she may not now be sure how much cricitism I can take.

Therapist: 'I was not helpful to you on this occasion, as you pointed out to me at the end of the last session. You had, after all, told me where I could obtain a copy of this tape without involving you; but instead I took the short-cut of borrowing it from you. That was a break in the usual relationship here, and it has been threatening to be harmful to your therapy unless this is recognized and properly dealt with. Otherwise, as with the tooth abscess, it could fester.'

Patient: 'That was another occasion when you surprised me: you said Dr X. must be a very good dentist for me to travel all this way to see him, and you then asked me for his name. It was so unlike you to ask, but again I felt it was good to be able to be helpful to you.'

Internal supervision: The patient points to each time she has felt that I have stepped out of role. She expresses a rationalized pleasure along with her surprise. The way in which she explains her pleasure includes an unconscious recognition of my having turned her into my helper, my unacknowledged therapist.

Therapist: 'So we have more than just one occasion when I can be seen as reversing roles with you, where you found yourself put into the position of having your own needs overlooked while you were being asked to attend to requests of mine. It may seem reassuring to find that I am human, and that you can be of help to me, but as far as your therapy is concerned this has led to a diversion from your reasons for coming to see me. I believe this is why you have been pointing out to me the contrast between people who do their jobs thoroughly and those who do not. When you pay me it is for me to do my job as therapist, and to do that carefully and attentively; not to have me sitting back and being social with you.'

I handed her the account, which she accepted with a knowing smile showing that she understood what I had just been saying to her. This was the end of the session.

The patient returned the following week feeling reassured by the work done in the session just quoted. She began to talk about the state of her marriage, and stresses in the family, that had been alluded to briefly before but she had felt unsure about discussing these in depth. Mrs A. confessed that she had begun to wonder whether there was any point in continuing with her therapy, but she was now relieved to find that it felt all right to go on. She was beginning to feel positive about her therapy again.

Discussion: Mrs A. demonstrates a degree of awareness of her therapist's state of mind that can be most disconcerting. Some people might wish to regard this as unusual, but it is probably typical. A patient will monitor the therapist either quite consciously (as some patients will point out) or unconsciously. Mrs A. has an intuitive grasp of what constitutes a secure framework for therapy. She notes every occasion when I crossed the boundaries necessary for insight-promoting psychotherapy. She unconsciously recognizes the counter-transference implications of these trangressions, and in the interests of her own therapy she contributes persistent unconscious supervisory efforts (Langs 1978) towards having these dealt with.

At the point in this clinical sequence when I was sliding into a state of 'countertransference neurosis' (Racker 1968) the patient shifted into the role of unconscious therapist to me (Searles 1975). Only when I began to recognize the outstanding breaks in the therapeutic boundaries did I start to listen around these as a primary issue to be attended to. It is this awareness that prompts me to focus my listening on the derivative rather than the manifest levels of the patient's communications, and that leads me eventually towards the necessary work of putting things right. As I begin to recover my role as therapist, the patient feels safe enough to point out other departures from the more usual therapeutic framework. When these are attended to, she is able to resume meaningful therapy.

Notes

1. I am indebted to Langs for prompting me to look more closely into this dimension of the therapeutic relationship. He speaks of 'the interactional-adaptational viewpoint', and sets out a detailed and systematic schema for listening (Langs 1978). I do not wish to describe that here. I wish only to outline an attitude to listening that includes an awareness of the patient's perception of the therapist's reality, and some responses to that reality.

2. The clinical account presented in this chapter is an extract from my paper 'The Reflective Potential of the Patient as Mirror to the Therapist'. In James O. Raney (ed.) (1984) *Listening and Interpreting: the Challenge of the Work of Robert Langs*, New York: Jason Aronson.

3. Marion Milner compares the function of the analytic frame to the part that is played by the frame of a picture in art:

> 'The frame marks off the different kind of reality that is within it from that which is outside it; but a temporal spatial frame also marks off the special kind of reality of a psycho-analytic session. And in psycho-analysis it is the existence of this frame that makes possible the full development of that creative illusion that analysts call transference.'
>
> (Milner 1952:183)

4

Forms of interactive communication

'It is a very remarkable thing that the *Ucs.* of one human being can react upon that of another, without passing through the *Cs.*' (Freud 1915:194)[1]

There are times when the most important communication from a patient is unspoken. The process of a therapist's internal supervision can often help to identify this interactive dimension, so that it begins to make sense. Patients clearly demonstrate that the dynamics involved are by no means just theoretical, nor are they confined to analytic therapy. The forms of communication illustrated here are universal. Too often they are not recognized or they are seen as bewildering: the communication then remains unacknowledged or not understood.

Communication by impact

Patients often behave in such a way that they stir up feelings in the therapist which could not be communicated in words. I have found it useful to consider this form of interaction under a general heading of communication by impact.

As a basic example of this, let us consider an infant's cry and the mother's response to its impact upon her. This is one of the most primitive ways by which one human being acts upon another, and is reacted to. A mother's response to her crying infant is usually to draw upon her maternal intuition, to sense the specific meaning of this particular cry. To that end she will often put herself empathically in the infant's position, or in her own mother's position when she herself was crying in a similar way, in order to distinguish between one kind of crying and another.

In psychotherapy, therapists are often subjected to the unspoken cries of those who come to consult them. As with the mother and her infant, therapists have to be able to listen within themselves to draw upon their own experience of distress (whether that had been contained or not). If therapists persevere in their wish to understand, even when they are experiencing the confusion or pain which some patients induce in them, times will occur when the unconscious purpose of these pressures becomes apparent.

Some patients need to be able to have this kind of effect on the therapist, as an essential way of communicating what otherwise may remain unspeakable. When a therapist is able to understand the unconscious purpose of communication by impact, and can find ways of interpreting this which help to make sense of it, then the patient can begin to feel that someone is really in touch with them – even with their own most difficult feelings.

Experiences relating to role-responsiveness

I shall not attempt to define this concept prior to giving an example.

Unconscious communication evoked through the therapist's response to the patient

Example 4.1

My first experience of being in any kind of supervisory role to another therapist was when I had just qualified as a psychotherapist. A colleague would sometimes let off steam to me by complaining about a particular patient of hers. This patient was described as coming from a good family, with parents who had maintained a good marriage, who had provided her with all that she could have needed in her childhood and in her education. The patient, however, was always complaining about her parents. She was described to me as 'so persistently ungrateful' that the therapist felt exasperated, and she wondered whether she could continue to work with her. The therapist could not see that there was anything to complain about.

Discussion: I was aware of the possibility that I was hearing a straightforward example of countertransference, such as my training had taught me to beware of. It could have been that the patient had become a transferential object to the therapist, representing some unresolved conflict of her own. What I knew of the therapist made me feel that this was not unlikely: I had gathered, from what she said about her family, that she sometimes thought of her own daughters as ungrateful.

Superficially, therefore, it looked as if there could hardly be a clearer example of countertransference, as it was first described (Freud 1910:144-45). I sensed that my colleague also thought of her response to this complaining patient as a countertransference problem, to be dealt with outside the patient's sessions. This may have been why she was venting her exasperation on me, in order not to off-load this onto her patient.

However, over a period of time, it began to dawn on me that my colleague could be missing an important communication, in this attitude which was so regularly being stimulated in her by this patient. The more I thought on this the more convinced I became that there was something else here, in addition to the classical phenomenon of countertransference.

The patient may have been unable to get across what it was about her parents that she was complaining of. Instead, she seemed to have *re-created in her therapist* the kind of attitude towards herself which her parents may have had. Perhaps they (like the therapist) had been blinded by an assumption that they had provided adequately for their daughter; and yet they may have been failing to recognize important ways in which they were shutting themselves off from the unmet needs of this complaining child. In order to communicate this, the patient might have been able to touch upon an available countertransference resonance in her therapist, thereby evoking *in her* similar feelings and attitudes to those of her parents. If this really were such a communication, it could be a way of picking up from the patient something of what her parents may have been missing, and which the therapist had been missing too.

So, instead of having to treat this strong response to the patient solely as something belonging elsewhere in the therapist's life (which in one sense it did), it could also be looked upon as conveying an intangible aspect of her relationship to her parents, about which she had been complaining. The parents had been shut off from this patient much as the therapist had come to be. Perhaps, in response to the patient's urgent need to get this across, the therapist had become involved in an unconscious re-enactment of the complained-of parents. In his paper 'Countertransference and Role-Responsiveness', Sandler was later to describe this process as 'actualization' (Sandler 1976).[2]

When I discussed this possibility with my colleague she was able to recognize the interactive communication here, which formerly she had been missing, and she started to listen to her patient differently. In so doing she became less shut off from the patient, and less caught up in her own feelings of intolerance towards her.

Heimann (1950) and Little (1951) have both pointed out that the analyst's feeling responses to the patient may contain valuable cues to the patient's unconscious communications. Sandler illustrated how the analyst can be drawn into a behavioural interaction. In 'Countertransference and Role-Responsiveness' he writes:

> 'I believe such "manipulations" to be an important part of object relationships in general.... In the transference, in many subtle ways, the patient attempts to prod the analyst into behaving in a particular way and unconsciously scans and adapts to his perceptions of the analyst's reaction.'

(Sandler 1976:44)

It is all the more important, therefore, that we should be able to distinguish that part of a therapist's responses which offers clues to the patient's unconscious communication from that which is personal to the therapist. In order to make this distinction, at the time of the clinical episode quoted, I suggested we might speak of a 'diagnostic response' as compared with a 'personal countertransference' (Casement 1973).

Boredom as communication

Example 4.2

For some months, in the course of a long analysis, I found myself regularly feeling bored by one particular male patient. I silently explored this as fully as I could to see if my feelings were simply some personal countertransference to my patient, as a transferential object, thinking here of countertransference in the sense described by Reich (1951). But even after this self-scrutiny, my feelings of boredom continued to occur in many of the sessions with this patient.

When I monitored this boredom more closely, I came to recognize I was responding to the fact that the patient was not relating to me. He seemed to be speaking to himself, as if I were not present; but this was not the whole of it. The patient treated me as physically present but emotionally absent. He was assuming that I was not interested, although this was not normally how I felt towards him. I could then see that the quality of his relating to me was as if to someone whose interest he could not engage, or who was unwilling to be engaged. This offered me a fresh clue.

What then stirred in me was a clear image of this patient at the time when he had been in a mental hospital. He had told me how his mother used to visit him regularly. She claimed to be concerned, and yet she continued to rationalize why her son had to remain in hospital. (He would have been allowed home if his parents had been prepared to look after him.)

The patient's presence in hospital was due to a prolonged agitated depression. This in turn was largely activated by the family's readiness to close ranks against this child, who had come to feel that life was not worth living. The parents did not seem to be prepared to let themselves be in touch with, or to be touched by, the patient's depression and despair – or by his need to be allowed home, rather than being left indefinitely in a mental hospital until he was 'better'. The parents were wanting to ignore the main reason for their son being left there. This was because he had nowhere else to go other than to his home, where his parents felt that they would not be able to cope with him in this chronic state.

With this re-activated memory as my cue, I began to wonder whether my patient might be re-enacting with me the empty relating that he had so often sat through while he remained in hospital. He had talked *at* his mother, who had barely listened. His mother, in her turn, had talked *at* him rather than *to* him.

When I began to re-focus my listening to the patient, in this new context, I could recognize many other indications which confirmed this impression. I became able to point out to the patient how he was speaking to me, as if he did not expect me really to be interested or to be ready to take seriously anything he said. I wondered whether this may have been how it used to be during his mother's visits to him in the hospital, which sounded as if they had been just as empty of meaningful relating.

Once I had been able to interpret this emptiness in the transference, the patient began to speak to me and to relate to me in a way that began (for the first time) to be invested with meaning. The transference stopped being a shallow relating, as if to a physically present but emotionally absent mother. Instead, the patient began to relate to me as to someone who was emotionally as well as physically present; and I stopped being troubled by boredom when I was with him.

An experience of projective identification

Although I had struggled to understand the concept of projective identification from what I had read about it, as in

Klein (1946) and Segal (1964) for example, it was not until I recognized being on the receiving end of this particular form of interactive communication that I began to understand it clinically. I shall again give an example before trying to conceptualize the dynamics illustrated.

Example 4.3

I was asked to see a couple, Mr and Mrs T., because of the wife's frigidity. They were both in their thirties. For the past five years Mrs T. had been unable to allow intercourse on account of what she described as 'gynaecological pain'. This had been causing great stress in the marriage. There was a serious risk of the couple splitting up.

Medical examinations and tests had revealed nothing, but the referring doctor had mentioned that Mrs T. had been sterilized three years earlier. He wondered whether this might have left post-operative adhesions. However, the gynaecologist thought that it would be pointless to re-open the operation scar, as this would probably only cause fresh adhesions. She could end up no better.

In the initial consultation I saw Mr and Mrs T. together, as they had been referred as a couple and had asked to come for help with their marriage. Mr T. took little part in this consultation. Mrs T., on the other hand, told me her story. They had been married about ten years, having known each other for several years before that. They had spent the first five years of the marriage getting a house and decorating it, in preparation for beginning a family.

After this introduction, Mrs T. told me about their two children. They had had a son and a daughter. She then told me the painful details of her discovery that there was something wrong with their first child. When he was six months old he began to scream continuously unless sedated. For nine months she nursed him until he died. Mrs T. was seven months pregnant with their second child at the time.

After attending the funeral of her son, she 'felt tearful but held it in'. She had never cried since then. She just felt numb. The second child, a daughter, was also born apparently normal. She died ten months later, of the same constitutional brain disorder as had her brother. It was after this that Mrs T. was advised to be sterilized.

Internal supervision: What was most striking, during the telling of this terrible sequence of pain and loss, was that Mrs T.'s face and tone of voice remained wooden and lifeless. Even when she was talking of the children's illness, and slow dying, she showed no feelings at all. But my own feelings, upon listening to her, were nearly overwhelming me. I was literally crying inside.

I wondered about my response. I knew I would be moved by any account of a child's death. Was this some personal countertransference problem, only to do with me? I had to consider this as a real possibility. But, as I looked into this further, I began to realize why I was being so affected. If Mrs T. had been crying her own tears I would not be feeling so overwhelmed. What was producing this effect upon me had something to do with her inability to show any expression of her own feelings.

I once again called upon my provisional concept of a diagnostic response. I postulated (to myself) that the intolerable pain of losing both her children in this way, followed by the sterilization (losing any chance of having other children of her own), had been too much for her. To survive these intolerable experiences, she may have converted the psychic pain belonging to them into gynaecological pain. Perhaps this symptom continued to express, somatically, the repressed feelings related to those unbearable losses, which had been so closely associated with that part of her body.

Mrs T. did much more than project her feelings onto me. She made *me* feel what *she* could not yet bear to feel consciously within herself. And the manner of this projection was not impossible to identify. I could see that it had been the patient's own lack of emotion that had been having the greatest impact upon me. As a result, I had been feeling in touch with tears which did not altogether belong to me.

After recognizing this response in myself I was able to draw Mrs T.'s attention to this. I said to her that there was something rather strange happening in the session. She had been telling me the details of her experience with her two children, but she had shown no feelings about this. I, on the other hand, had felt near to tears *as if for her*. She replied that she frequently needed to talk about the death of her children, but people had begged her not to as it affected them in much the same way as I had just described. She had relied upon not feeling anything about these experiences. It would probably be too painful. Instead she had kept herself active, to keep her mind occupied with other things.

Discussion: I felt sure that, if Mrs T. could be helped to be in touch with her own crying inside, perhaps to be able to cry openly instead, she would not need her body to continue to be in pain. The subsequent course of her brief therapy fully confirmed this diagnostic impression. As she became able to bear to be in touch with the previously repressed psychic pain, her gynaecological pains began to fade away. She was able to enter into the process of mourning which had been so long delayed.

Projective identification as communication

Unfortunately, it is not easy to get a clear understanding of projective identification from the literature alone, as this concept has become complicated by the varied uses to which it has been put.[3] However, through the above experience and others like it, I became able to recognize clinically a part of what projective identification is about – how it happens and the unconscious purpose of it.

One of the uses of projective identification that many people experience clinically (whether they know it or not) is a form of affective communication.[4] This is especially relevant when what is being communicated is beyond words, relating to unspeakable experiences or to pre-verbal experience.

In order that therapists (and those in the other helping

professions) may be more able to respond therapeutically when they encounter this form of unconscious communication, I shall endeavour to clarify this particular aspect of projective identification. I shall not discuss the other forms of this here, but I refer briefly to these in the footnotes. My description will therefore be incomplete, but I trust that it will be clear enough to encourage therapists to recognize the importance and implications of this key interactional dynamic. With the help of this understanding, it becomes possible to contain some patients who might otherwise remain uncontained. Without it, the meaning of the helper's feelings of stress may be misunderstood, and some patients will not find the help they look for. This frequently results in missed opportunities for better understanding of patients in distress.

I find it helpful to think of projective identification as a more powerful form of projection. It is well known that when projection (simple) is operating, the projector disowns some aspect of the self and attributes this to another. Evidence of that projection is usually to be noticed in the projector relating differently to the other person (or outside world) in terms of what has been projected. The recipient, or observer, may otherwise be quite unaware of any projection operating. What is foremost here is the projector's need to disown some aspect of himself.

When projective identification is used *as a form of affective communication*, the projector has a need (usually unconscious) to make another person aware of what is being communicated and to be responded to. The sequence is roughly as follows: (1) the projector experiences unmanageable feelings, such as an infant might have; (2) there is an unconscious phantasy of putting this unmanageable feeling-state into another person, such as the mother, for this to be disposed of or made manageable; (3) there is an interactional pressure, such as an infant's cry, with the unconscious aim of making the *other* person have these feelings instead of the infant or patient; (4) if this communication by projective identification is successful in reaching the other person, an affective resonance is created in the recipient whose feelings take on a 'sameness' based on identification. This affective identification can then be thought of as being brought about projectively by the projector and introjectively by the recipient.

There are several different possible results to this unconscious endeavour. If the recipient is open to the impact of the interactional behaviour, or other non-verbal pressures from the projector, an affective communication is achieved. What is communicated may be to do with any state of feeling that is experienced as unmanageable by the projector; acute distress, helplessness, fear, rage, contemptuous attack upon the self, etc. The feelings being communicated are felt by the recipient.

What is then needed (for a therapeutic response to be possible) is for the recipient, the mother or the therapist, to be more able to manage being in touch with these feelings than the infant or patient had been. When this response is found, the previously unmanageable feelings become more manageable. They become less terrifying than before, because another person has actually felt them and has been able to tolerate the experience of those feelings. The projector can thereafter take back those feelings, now made more manageable; and along with this can take in something of the recipient's capacity to tolerate being in touch with difficult feelings. The unconscious hope, implied in the use of projective identification as communication, thereby meets a therapeutic response from the mother or therapist.

However, this unconscious hope is not always met. For example, if the recipient remains shut off from this attempt at communication or fails to recognize the interactive pressures as a form of communication, there will be no therapeutic response. The projector then experiences the projection as thrown back; and the unmanageable feelings being projected remain unmanageable. Likewise, if the recipient experiences (but cannot bear being subjected to) the feelings being projected, the projector will experience the recipient as thrown off balance by what is being projected; and the sense of these feelings being unmanageable is traumatically confirmed. Instead of the unconscious hope being met, there is a new state of hopelessness and despair (Bion 1967b:Chapter 9).

In Chapter Seven I present a clinical sequence which illustrates these issues more extensively.

Communication through defensive behaviour

One way of seeking refuge from the pain of being badly treated is to identify with the aggressor and to treat another person in a similar way, thereby inducing in someone else the unwanted pain of that experience (A. Freud 1937). There are times when a patient will unconsciously re-create in a therapist feelings that belong to the experience in question, and which the patient is trying to 'get rid of' in this way. It is therefore not only unmanageable feeling-states that come to be evoked in the therapist by means of impact behaviour; this may include aspects of the patient's unbearable experience. (Kleinians would probably regard this too as a form of projective identification.)

If a therapist recognizes when he is being subjected to this kind of interactive pressure from a patient, it is often possible to find a clue to such unconscious communication in his own affective response to the patient's behaviour (see King 1978).

Example 4.4

A patient, during the early stages of an analysis, noticed that I had been using my library (which is an integral part of my consulting room). I had been looking up references for some work I was doing, and I had not tidied up after pulling out books and journals from the shelves.

The patient said he could not live with his books in such a state of mess. He would want to have the books all in order, and he wondered how I could put up with my shelves like that, day after day.

That evening I thought about the dilemma that I felt placed in. I wanted to tidy my shelves; but if I did this straight away the patient could feel that he had made me tidy them, and I felt uneasy about it looking as if I had obediently done what I had been told to do. Of course, I could avoid that discomfort by leaving everything as it was; but I still wanted to tidy the shelves.

For a while I felt paralysed by this apparently trivial issue. The only solution was to do what made most sense to me. I

tidied the books; but, when I came to the journals that I had
not finished using, there remained an element of the same
dilemma. Again, I did what suited me. I left the unfinished
journals on their side, lying over books on the shelf.

When the patient came to his next session he looked at the
changes on the shelves. After some thought, he exploded in
a tone of voice quite unlike anything I had heard from him
before: 'PATHETIC!' After a silence he elaborated further.
He thought that I could not have chosen a more ridiculous
compromise. He said if I didn't want to feel pushed around
by him it would have been better to have left the shelves as
they were. Perhaps I liked them like that. If, on the other
hand, I actually wanted to tidy them why on earth not finish
the job? As it was, he concluded, I had left a few journals not
tidied away as a 'token gesture of independence'. Why
hadn't I just done what I wanted to do?

Internal supervision: As I thought about the patient's perception of what he saw as my compromise, I realized I had been in
a double-bind after his last session. This had seemed insoluble
until I chose to resolve it in the only way that allowed me to be
free. I had done what had suited me, leaving out the journals I
was still working on. The patient expected me to have
remained in the double-bind, not able to resolve it. He also
assumed that I could not let myself do what I wanted to do.

I began to realize the significance of this interaction. It had
already become clear, in the short period of his analysis so far,
that this patient had been regularly placed in double-binds by
his mother; and he had not been able to find a way out of the
paralysis which that behaviour induced in him.

I said I thought the issue was about being in a double-bind,
and I told him that I had been aware of being in a dilemma
about tidying the shelves. He was right in supposing I
wanted to tidy them; but he also assumed I had been
unable to do what I wanted. I thought that this assumption
was because he had so often not been able to cope with
similar double-binds from his mother. He had not found a
way out of that through doing what *he* wanted to do.

The patient recognized what I was describing. He said his mother was probably 'the double-binding mother of all time'. Whatever he did, his mother always found some way of saying it was all wrong. He had never found any way of dealing with this. He also agreed he had been doing to me the kind of thing his mother used to do to him, but he could not see that I had found any way of dealing with his double-binding of me.

I told him I was still using the journals which were not put away, so I had kept these out. Equally, I wanted to tidy the rest and I was glad to have been prompted to get round to this.

What followed helped us to see that the patient had been unconsciously testing me. He was relieved to know I had felt double-bound. He also thought it was no accident he had selected an issue of untidiness. His mother had frequently made him tidy up, or clean; and he could never satisfy her. There was always something his mother would criticize him for, however careful or thorough he was.

Discussion: In this unconscious interaction, the patient had been doing to me the kind of thing his mother had so often done to him. (The defensive behaviour here was that of identification with the aggressor.) Through my response to his pressures I had felt something of what he used to feel from his mother. This helped me to recognize what it could have been like for him as a child, with his mother. He was subsequently able to discover that he too could do what made sense to himself, rather than remain constantly paralysed by trying to please his unpleasable mother; and he began to establish a separateness from her which he had never before dared to attempt.

A countertransference response to imminent stress in the analysis

Example 4.5

A patient, who was leading up to a crisis in her analysis, had been expressing her fear of 'going to pieces or going mad',

and how she might be left permanently vulnerable because of that experience. Also, she might never really
recover from it.

Without recognizing why at the time, I acted upon a
countertransference impulse – meaning to help this patient
find the courage not to run away from what she was fearing.
I mistakenly told her I had found that a lasting strength for
me had grown out of daring to face my own deepest fears,
even the fears of going to pieces or of going mad.

The patient read my comment (at some level quite
correctly) as expressing unconscious anxiety of my own.
She took this to mean that I was warning her not to go further
into this experience in her analysis.

Internal supervision: It would, of course, have been far better if
I had continued to analyse the patient's anxiety about whether
I could help her through the experience that she feared. By
resorting to this non-analytic procedure I am failing to hold
her analytically at this moment.

Now, quite apart from any transference implications for the
patient, it is likely she will need me to attend to the reality basis
for her subsequent fears. She gave me clear confirmation of
this need in her next session.

> *Patient:* 'I had a terrible dream:
> *I was going up a mountain in a cable-car. Suddenly it*
> *broke down and stopped. I was stuck half-way up the*
> *mountain, unable to go any further and unable to go*
> *back. I was stranded. What made it much worse was that*
> *the door of the cable-car kept on swinging open. It was*
> *all glass in a metal frame – a casement frame.'*

Internal supervision: I was hearing of the patient's journey
being in jeopardy from something that had broken down. The
day residue referred to in this dream seemed obvious: there
was a door swinging open, and the frame of the cable-car was
made of glass (too transparent). The frame that she described
is (in England) called a 'casement frame'.

I was immediately reminded of the analytic frame and of what I had told her about myself, in trying to tell her that I was familiar with the kind of experience she feared. I realized this was now causing her to be fearful for her analysis.

> *Analyst:* 'I cannot fail to see the references to what I told you about myself, and my familiarity with the experience of going to pieces. This has not helped. Instead, it has made you anxious about whether I can cope with what may lie ahead in your analysis – so anxious that you seem to be wondering whether you can even dare to continue your analysis with me.'
>
> *Patient:* 'I feel you are warning me not to go any further towards that experience. In fact, I think you are telling me you might not be able to cope. Perhaps you do feel threatened and need to warn me not to go on. But I also can't go back.'

What followed during this session, and the sessions after it, was a period of acute anxiety with the patient having to test and re-test my capacity to hold her analytically through whatever was still to come in her analysis. She went into an intensely frightening sequence of sessions, during which she eventually did experience herself as 'going to pieces'. She also dreamed of her foundations breaking up, as if from an earthquake. But she did not get into this re-living of her childhood experience of disintegration until after we had done the necessary analytic work on her dream, which so clearly showed the implications for her in my attempt at reassuring her and the need for me to recover my analytic holding of the patient.

Discussion: In this sequence, I had to accept that I had provoked what followed in the analysis. But I do not think this accounts for it all.

The patient had already indicated she felt there was a crisis brewing up for her. When she later experienced going to pieces in the analysis, the sense of her foundations being threatened was no doubt linked with what I had introduced in the analysis, by the uncalled-for element of self-exposure. Nevertheless, I do not think this patient would have been able to go on with her analysis if what followed was entirely caused by my break in the analytic frame, which usually preserves the relative anonymity of the analyst from intruding upon the analytic process. The dreaded experience also belonged in her own early life-experience, and had to be lived through in the analysis before she could deal with her own 'fear of break-down' (Winnicott 1970).

Comment: I have noticed that several times, and with different patients, I have fallen into a sequence similar to the one above. There is no doubt that some countertransference is always operating when I deflect a patient, or try to reassure, particularly as I know so well that this does not work. So why does it keep on happening?

It occurred to me during the later session, when this patient told me of her earthquake dream, that I had recently heard about areas in the world where earthquakes are common. Apparently it has been noticed there that animals start to behave strangely, dogs barking and geese cackling, shortly before there is an earthquake. It is the usual practice, in such regions, to seize the children and to get them into the open (for safety) in case there is an earthquake threatening.

Perhaps there is a similar function performed by the countertransference: but in this case (and in others) I had missed the moment of recognition. I now think that the impulse to reassure is not just an important cue for caution. Sometimes it may also be an early pointer to some kind of earthquake-experience which may be imminent in the analysis or therapy. So, if we could listen to this impulse to reassure, like those people who respond to the early warnings they receive from animals, we could be better prepared for what may follow.

One further encounter with the interactive unconscious that I wish to describe, relates to Winnicott's concept of the patient's use of the analyst's failures. He writes of this in a number of different places (e.g. Winnicott 1958: Chapter 22; 1965b: Chapter 23).

A therapist's failure and the patient's past history

Example 4.6

A therapist was seeing a patient in three-times-a-week psychotherapy. The patient (whom I shall call Miss G.) had been traumatized as a child by her mother's repeated absences, in hospital with cancer, and (at the age of four) by her mother's death.

From the beginning of this treatment the therapist was kept firmly engaged by this needy patient, even though Miss G. frequently failed to turn up for sessions; and for a long time her silence at the beginning of sessions had exerted an enormous pressure on the therapist to speak first.

In this phase of the treatment the therapist listened closely to what she was thinking and feeling, during these silences or unexplained absences. She realized she was left not knowing what was happening to the patient, and (on some occasions) she even wondered whether she would ever see Miss G. again.

Over a period of time the therapist came to wonder whether her patient was making her feel a sense of abandonment and uncertainty, similar to that which Miss G. had probably felt during her mother's unexplained absences in hospital, and after her eventual death. This is another example of communication by impact, the therapist responding to the powerful effects on her caused by the patient's absences and/or silences.

Listening to what the patient was making her feel in this way, the therapist was able to interpret to Miss G. her awareness of how unbearable it must have been when she was so often left in this state of not knowing what was happening to her mother, and what had later happened when she never saw her again. The patient was gradually able to acknowledge that this made sense to her. It also helped her to forego most of her opening silences in sessions; though, at times of deepest despair, she would again resort to lateness (or absence) now knowing that this would be understood by her therapist as a sign of distress.

Comment: We can see here how Miss G. was able to communicate feelings which were beyond words, but which had been heard and understood because of the impact they made on the therapist. The therapist made good use of her knowledge of the dynamics of projective identification, and the patient remained in therapy even through times of greatest despair. The therapist also understood how important it was to Miss G. that she (the therapist) should be regularly there for the sessions, whether the patient came or not. Regularity, reliability, and on-going constancy were carefully maintained by this therapist for her patient.

> One morning the therapist overslept.[5] The patient came to the therapist's consulting room for her early morning session, only to find herself shut out. She remained outside the locked door until the cleaner arrived. For the rest of her session time she was looked after by this cleaner, who expressed particular concern about the therapist's absence as it was 'so unlike her not to be here'. Inevitably, Miss G. felt something really serious must have happened. Perhaps there had been an accident. Perhaps her therapist was in hospital. Maybe she had died.

Discussion: The patient's experience of separation and her increased need of the absent mother had come to be deeply linked in her mind. So, after her mother's death Miss G. began to believe that it could have been the intensity of her need for her mother that had caused her to leave, and eventually to die. In the therapy itself there had now come to be a dramatic repetition of this same sequence, which clearly demonstrated her phantasy that it might be her dependency and need which 'caused' the person she depended upon to be absent, perhaps to have become ill or to have died.

It is uncanny how this therapist unconsciously reproduced a real failure in the therapy which was so close to the experience of her patient's own childhood trauma. How is it, then, that we sometimes fail a patient even when we are so carefully trying not to? When this happens it can threaten the whole therapeutic relationship. And yet, when a patient is confronted by a real issue like this, about which he or she can be genuinely angry with the therapist in the present, it can equally become a pivotal experience in the therapy.

It could be that any re-creation of an earlier trauma in the therapy comes about partly through an interplay of personal countertransference and role-responsiveness. Winnicott, however, speaks of a further dimension to this unconscious interaction:

> 'Corrective provision is never enough. What is it that may be enough for some of our patients to get well? In the end the patient uses the analyst's failures, often quite small ones, perhaps manoeuvred by the patient ... and we have to put up with being in a limited context misunderstood. The operative factor is that the patient now hates the analyst for the failure that originally came as an environ-mental factor, outside the infant's area of omnipotent control but that is *now* staged in the transference. So in the end we succeed by failing – failing the patient's way. This is a long distance from the simple theory of cure by corrective experience.'
>
> (Winnicott 1965b:258)

Later, in relation to his own patient in this paper, Winnicott adds: 'I must not fail in the child-care and infant-care aspects of the treatment until at a later stage when *she will make me fail* in ways determined by her history (Winnicott 1965b:258-59).

Miss G. may have unconsciously prompted her therapist to fail her 'in ways determined by her history'. So, at a time when she was being sensitively and consistently held in the thera-peutic relationship (with unconscious reminders of a good holding-relationship that had existed earlier with her mother), this therapist became involved in a real failure of her patient. The nature of this failure had a terrifying similarity for the patient to her own childhood trauma. She consequent-ly experienced, in the present with her therapist, her own obliterating anger that belonged to the original trauma.

The patient was able to find in this experience a real opportunity to *use* her therapist to represent the mother who had 'failed' her, who had inexplicably shut her out by not being there. She could now begin to attack her therapist with her own strongest feelings about that earlier (and this present) failure, with her therapist surviving these attacks of rage upon her.

In his paper 'Use of an Object and Relating through Identification', Winnicott stresses that the key to this survival, is to be found in the patient discovering that the analyst (or therapist) has a strength that is not 'created' by the patient's phantasy or projection (Winnicott 1971:Chapter 6). Miss G. could only begin to modify her unconscious phantasy, that it had been her own anger at her mother's absences which had seemed to have been the cause of her death, through subjecting her therapist to her most intense feelings about that absence with her therapist (ultimately) not retaliating or collapsing, but surviving.

Various aspects of countertransference

If we are to suppose, as I do here, that there is a level of communication which is achieved through some interactive responsiveness between patient and therapist, it is essential that there should be ways of distinguishing between different kinds of response to the patient.

A great deal has been written on this. I shall not, however, endeavour to offer any systematic review of the literature on countertransference. This has been done thoroughly by others.[6] I wish only to outline some of the different ways in which countertransference has been written about, in particular those ways which throw light upon the examples given above.

(1) Countertransference can be regarded as 'a result of the patient's influence on his [the physician's] unconscious feelings' (Freud 1910:145), for which the analyst should use self-analysis to resolve or seek further analytic help.

(2) M. Balint (1933:Chapter 12) and A. Reich (1951), likewise, both emphasized the fact that there are times when an analyst experiences a *transference response* to the patient. This can occur when a patient comes to represent some unresolved aspect of a significant relationship in the earlier life of the analyst or

therapist; and this will threaten therapeutic work with that patient unless it is resolved through further self-analysis of the therapist.

(3) Winnicott, in his provocative paper 'Hate in the Countertransference', refers to a truly objective countertransference. For instance, he says: 'A main task of the analyst of any patient is to maintain objectivity in regard to all that the patient brings, and a special case of this is the analyst's need to be able to hate the patient objectively' (Winnicott 1958:196). And later he adds:

> 'The analyst's hate is ordinarily latent and is easily kept so. In analysis of psychotics the analyst is under greater strain to keep his hate latent, and he can only do this by being thoroughly aware of it. I want to add that in certain stages of certain analyses the analyst's hate is actually sought by the patient, and what is then needed is hate that is objective. If the patient seeks objective or justified hate he must be able to reach it, else he cannot feel he can reach objective love.'
>
> (Winnicott 1958:199)

(4) Paula Heimann stressed the 'counter-' part of countertransference, seeing this as the analyst's response to the patient's transference. She emphasized that: 'the analyst's emotional response to his patient within the analytic situation represents one of the most important tools for his work. The analyst's counter-transference is an instrument of research into the patient's unconscious' (Heimann 1950:81). She later continues:

> 'I would suggest that the analyst along with this freely working attention needs a freely roused emotional sensibility so as to follow the patient's emotional movements and unconscious phantasies. Our basic assumption is that the analyst's unconscious understands that of his patient. This rapport on the deep level comes to the surface in the form of feelings which the analyst notices in response to his patient, in his "counter-transference". This is the

most dynamic way in which his patient's voice reaches
him.'

(Heimann 1950:82)

(5) Pearl King, in her paper 'Affective Response of the
Analyst to the Patient's Communications', tries to get free of
the confusingly different uses of countertransference:

'It is thus of central importance to distinguish between
countertransference as a pathological phenomenon and
the affective response of the analyst to the patient's
communications, particularly his affective response to
the various forms that the patient's transference takes.'

(King 1978:330)

What belongs to whom?

What most writers agree upon, in their differing ways, is that
therapists are affected by their patient's impacts upon them,
whether this be due to a patient's personality, a patient's
transference, or a patient's manner of being. Often, the
therapist's response to this may indicate something that has
only to do with the therapist. At times, there may be elements
also of unconscious communication from the patient. It
cannot always be rigidly defined as countertransference or
not, as pathological or not.

Once it is accepted that there can be an interactive communication between patient and therapist, a number of
technical issues are immediately raised. I wish to concentrate
on problems relating to the question: 'whose pathology is
operating at any given moment, the patient's or the therapist's,
and how can we distinguish one from the other?'

Even after a personal analysis, any therapist is still liable to
use the defences of projection and denial, particularly when
under pressure. So, the first step must be to monitor one's
feelings, in any therapeutic interaction, for personal countertransference. Even though this may be triggered by something
about the patient, a therapist must first accept what belongs to
himself. The next step is to determine whether a patient is

prompting the therapist to feel or to respond in a given way, and if so how and to what unconscious end might that be?

The therapist's resonance to the patient

A therapist's receptivity to the patient's unconscious communication becomes manifest in his resonance to interactive pressures. This resonance results from a matching between what is personal to the therapist and what comes from the patient. How responsive a therapist can be to patients, at this interactive level of feeling compared with cognitive understanding, will depend upon two things in particular about the therapist.

First, he or she needs to have access to these unconscious resonances across as wide a range of feeling as possible. Therapists do not have to remain limited to their own experiences, their own ways of being and feeling. It is possible that each person carries the potential to feel all feelings and to resonate to all experiences, however strange or alien these may be to their conscious selves; but, whenever there are unresolved areas of repression or continued disavowal, there will continue to be degrees of feeling that remain deadened and unresponsive. The expanding of a therapist's range of empathic resonance is a major gain from analysis, and this needs to be a continuing process.

Second, every therapist has to learn to be open to the 'otherness' of the other – being ready to feel whatever feelings result from being in touch with another person, however different that person is from themselves. Empathic identification is not enough, as it can limit a therapist to seeing what is familiar, or is similar to his own experience. Therapists therefore have to develop an openness to, and respect for, feelings and experiences that are quite unlike their own. The greater freedom they have to resonate to the unfamiliar 'keys' or dissonant 'harmonics' of others, the more it will enhance their receptivity to these unconsciously interactive cues that are often central to an understanding of patients.

A review of the examples

In the examples given we can see different admixtures of what belongs to the therapist and what comes from the patient.

The therapist who complained about an ungrateful patient was aware of a similarity between the patient and her daughters. This awareness prompted her to be cautious, but this caution also inhibited her. Once she could recognize that her resonance to the patient's ingratitude was also a response to something from her patient, she could begin to see that her attitude to the patient had become similar to that of her patient's parents.

My boredom, with the second patient, did not lift however much I looked for reasons within myself. Once I recognized a similarity between that analytic relationship and an empty kind of relating in this patient's earlier life, I was able to understand the feelings that this patient had so regularly engendered within me.

When I was with the woman whose children had died, the intensity of my feelings might have belonged only to me. Once again, however, the patient's contribution to my response (in the absence of her own feelings) led me to be confident that there was also an unconscious communication through her evoking those feelings in me.

The fourth example, when I tidied my bookshelves, is different. I was placed in a situation in which I could not do right in the patient's eyes. Here the feeling was of being trapped, or paralysed, which helped me to recognize that the patient had unconsciously manoeuvred me so that, whatever I did, I could not escape cricitism – even ridicule. I had a hunch that the patient may have been identifying with his mother, placing me in a situation similar to that which he had experienced in childhood. It was only possible to explore this possibility by sharing with the patient my perception of that experience, and how I had set about resolving it.

One factor which these four examples have in common is that we are able to identify, in each, some contribution from the patient towards the therapist's responses. This is important because, if we can see what evokes these responses to the patient, we are on surer ground when we postulate that there may be some communication being conveyed by means of this interactive behaviour.

In the fifth example, when I tried to reassure the patient, I was clearly responding to some unconscious anxiety about what lay ahead in this patient's analysis. This could have been more clearly anticipated if I had recognized the diagnostic element in my countertransference response to the patient. Consciously I felt well equipped and prepared for what lay ahead. Unconsciously I responded like those animals that sense an imminent earthquake.

The last example is more problematic. One view could be to regard this therapist's oversleeping simply as an acting out against the patient. We must not ignore this possiblity. My impression, however, is that it becomes more meaningful when this is also considered as a further example of interactive communication. I find Winnicott's theoretical statements about a patient's use of the analyst's failures convincing, but I acknowledge that it would be wrong for any therapist to shelter behind this as a way of denying his own part in failures encountered in an analysis or therapy.

The issue of intensity

An interesting idea, which seems to be missed by other writers, arises from this notion of interactive communication. If it is valid to think of patients using communication by impact or projective identification, as a means whereby the unspeakable can be conveyed to the therapist, then there will be times when the feelings involved are going to be very intense. Sometimes it may be the *intensity* that is the main point of the communication. So, if therapists are to be adequately in touch with this, they will find themselves also experiencing feelings with a similar intensity.

In contrast to this, Heimann describes the more usual view when she says:

> 'Since... violent emotions of any kind, of love or hate, helpfulness or anger, impel towards action rather than towards contemplation and blur a person's capacity to

observe and weigh the evidence correctly, it follows that,
if the analyst's emotional response is intense, it will defeat
its object .... The analyst's emotional sensitivity needs to
be extensive rather than intensive, differentiating and
mobile.'

(Heimann 1950:82)

My experience with patients has led me to disagree with this
view. The analyst or therapist has to learn to tolerate being in
touch with violent emotions so that they do not 'impel towards
action', rather than to suppress these feelings. And, when the
capacity for clear contemplation or observation is blurred, the
possible communication in this too should be looked for when
sufficient clarity of thinking has been recovered.

The use and mis-use of countertransference in interpretation

Some therapists interpret almost directly from their own
feelings about the patient; but if a therapist says to a patient
(for example), 'You are making me feel...', this can suggest
that all responsibility for what the therapist is feeling is being
placed upon the patient.

Similarly, it is unwise to subject a patient to samples of
self-analysis when trying to understand (or to explain) some
erroneous interpretation, or other disturbing activity by the
therapist. That should be the therapist's private affair.
Heimann therefore said that there should be no confessions by
the analyst to the patient. However, she was clear that: 'The
emotions aroused in the analyst will be of value to his patient, if
used as one more source of insight into the patient's unconscious conflicts and defences' (Heimann 1950:83-4).

Margaret Little on the other hand, considers that there are
occasions when it can be of great benefit to a patient if the
analyst is open about *some* of his or her feelings:

'In the later stages of analysis then, when the patient's
capacity for objectivity is already increased, the analyst
needs especially to be on the look-out for countertransference manifestations, and for opportunities to

interpret it, whether directly or indirectly, as and when the patient reveals it to him. Without it patients may fail to recognize objectively much of the irrational parental behaviour which has been so powerful a factor in the development of the neurosis, for wherever the analyst does behave like the parents, and conceals the fact, there is the point at which continued repression of what might otherwise be recognized is inevitable.'

(Little 1951:38)

The above examples illustrate some occasions when a cautious honesty about feelings evoked by a patient can enable the therapeutic process. This is less likely to be intrusive if we can identify the patient's contribution to this, as for instance in example 4.3 where I told the patient about the suppressed crying.

However, when it is not yet clear whether there is any real communication from the patient in the therapist's responses, the patient should not be burdened with uncalled-for evidence of what the therapist is feeling. I can illustrate this most easily from example 4.2. There, I did not think it fitting to tell the patient that I was feeling bored. So, rather than interpret direct from the countertransference (which is always inadvisable) I was able to listen more alertly; and from that new alertness I could begin to recognize the empty relating which had been so powerfully acting upon me to evoke this boredom.

It is a sound principle that countertransference should not intrude upon the analytic process; but this should not deter us from using our resonance to the patient to aid our further listening. Any subsequent interpretation that is based upon interactive communication needs to be linked to some identifiable cues from the patient, that he or she can recognize when made aware of them. When we cannot identify these cues, this usually indicates that there are not yet sufficient grounds for an interpretation if it is arrived at solely through the therapist's responses to the patient.

Notes

1. Earlier in the same paper, Freud wishes to distiguish between: 'using the words "conscious" and "unconscious" sometimes in a descriptive and sometimes in a systematic sense, in which latter they signify inclusion in particular systems and possession of certain charateristics' (Freud 1915:172).

He later goes on to say:

> 'Perhaps we may look for some assistance from the proposal to employ, at any rate in writing, the abbreviation *Cs.* for consciousness and *Ucs.* for what is unconscious, when we are using the two words in the systematic sense.'
>
> (Freud 1915:172)

2. A similar description of this process is give by Wangh (1962), in which he speaks of 'the "Evocation of a Proxy"'.

3. Projective identification as a concept is variously used to describe aspects of early psychic development in the infant (Klein 1952; Segal 1964), a primitive form of communication (Bion 1967b, for example), and for describing psychotic processes (Rosenfeld 1965; Bion 1967b). I am aware of the emphasis that Kleinians put upon splitting as involved in projective identification, but I am not including this in my present discussion of this concept. Projective identification is also used differently by Kleinians and other analysts, as discussed by Grotstein (1981) and Ogden (1982).

4. Rosenfeld (1971) distinguishes between projective identification used for communication and projective identification used for ridding the self of unwanted parts. He adds a third use of this, where the psychotic patient aims at controlling the analyst's body and mind. He points out that this seems to be based on a very early infantile type of object relationship. He also emphasizes that these three types of projective identification exist simultaneously in the psychotic patient, and that it is important not to concentrate on one form of this process alone when dealing with psychotics. (I am confining myself here to considering the use of projective identification by non-psychotics.)

5. Lucia Tower gives a similar example, in her paper 'Countertransference', in which she forgot a patient's session. This prompted her to recognize that her repressed irritation with this patient had been maintained by a reaction formation of 'infinite patience'. She adds that a denied negative countertransference can at times result in 'a negative countertransference structure, virtually a short-lived countertransference neurosis', unless something precipitates the necessary resolution of this which her own acting out against her patient helped to bring about (Tower 1956:238).

6. See, for instance, Orr (1954), Kernberg (1965), Laplanche and Pontalis (1973), Sandler, Dare and Holder (1973), Epstein and Feiner (1979).

5

Listening from an interactional viewpoint: a clinical presentation

In the last chapter I gave an example of a therapist re-enacting a traumatic element of the patient's childhood experience (Miss G. in example 4.6), where it was possible that this re-enactment grew out of the therapist's unconscious response to unconscious cues from the patient. I shall give here a more detailed illustration from an analysis in which, during the reported sequence, similar dynamics gradually emerged.

I also use this clinical sequence as a further illustration of learning to use internal supervision. I therefore follow the analytic process at three levels: (1) the analytical dialogue – what the patient and I said, in sequence, in each session; (2) internal supervision – what I was thinking, in the session, and how I arrived at each intervention; (3) hindsight – a commentary on some of what I later realized I had missed at each point in the session. Much of this hindsight occurred to me when writing notes after each session. I selected this particular week for making fuller notes than usual because I knew I was currently having difficulties in this analysis, and I was trying to sort out what was happening.

We will see that I made a number of mistakes in this sequence, which at the time seemed quite inexplicable. Gradually I began to recognize, and to respond to, the patient's unconscious cues which helped me to recover an analytic holding in the analysis. The following day, the patient made a surprising use of this recovery, re-experiencing in the session a very early trauma. With hindsight, some of those 'mistakes' could then be understood from a dynamically different perspective.

Background to the week of sessions to be presented[1]

Mrs B. was in the third year of her analysis. (This patient has been referred to already in Chapter One, example 1.5.) She was about thirty when she started treatment, at which time she had not been long married. She had given birth to a son, here called Peter, six months prior to the week that follows. Before her pregnancy with Peter, the analysis had focused mainly on an accident that had occurred when Mrs B. was eleven months old. She had pulled boiling water onto herself, while her mother was busy elsewhere, and had been severely burned. This experience was worked over repeatedly during the analysis, in dreams and in many sessions, but it had remained as a memory never to be consciously remembered.

After her son's birth Mrs B. became healthily preoccupied with being a mother, the accident shifting largely into the background of the analysis; and having begun to feel much better, she suggested dropping her Friday sessions. Peter was beginning to wean himself, and (as it seemed) so was she. Mrs B. also told me she was offering flexibility to Peter, for him to be able to move away from her – with her still there when he needed her. Therefore, when she showed anxiety about losing her fifth session permanently, I wondered if she had been prompting me to offer her a similar flexibility. As a result I offered her a compromise arrangement. I agreed to keep her usual Friday time available for a month or two, during which period she ould see how it felt to be coming only four times per week. Then, when Mrs B. showed concern about my wanting to use that time for another patient, I told her I would be using it for myself, for reading. She seemed pleased and grateful for this offer; but, as soon as she began coming less frequently, her anxiety mounted. The week I shall now present is the fourth week with this reduced frequency of sessions.

Hindsight: We can see that I have interrupted the analytic process in a number of ways. Rather than analysing the un-resolved anxiety about dropping this session, I have presented myself in the role of a good mother, offering a flexible weaning. This appears to gratify the patient but it more clearly meets a need of my own. The patient prompts me to re-consider my offer. She could be indicating the inappropriateness of the flexible arrangement, but I fail to recognize her cue. Instead I rationalize my offer by telling her how I plan to use the Friday time. I thereby give her valid grounds for perceiving me as wanting a rest from seeing her so often.

The clinical sequence

Monday

The patient began the session by saying she had had a mixed weekend. She felt it was possible she was not yet ready to drop her Friday sessions. (Pause.) She had had two dreams. In the first: *a girl was looking after a cat that had had a kitten. She had helped this cat deliver the kitten, which was lying in a pool of blood. The kitten was too weak to survive and died.* In her associations Mrs B. told me she had a friend whose daughter had the same name as the girl in the dream. (I shall call her Emma.) 'Emma has a white kitten. This kitten has a scratch that won't heal.' On saying this, Mrs B. became very distressed. (Pause.)

Internal supervision: The patient seems to identify herself with the kitten in the dream. I note the references to 'too weak to survive' and 'a scratch that won't heal'. I also note that the primary concern seems to have been announced at the beginning of the session when she said she was not yet ready to drop the Friday sessions. I therefore choose to interpret with this issue as my focus.

I said I had the impression she was anxious about dropping the fifth session, partly because she was afraid she might not be inwardly strong enough to cope with the change, and she might be afraid I would assume from such a change that the emotional scars had healed more than perhaps they had. The patient agreed with this interpretation and told me the other dream. *She had been swimming very slowly in a pool.* She had no associations.

Internal supervision: I believe this dream is offered as confirmation of her need to go slowly, and I prepare to acknowledge that I have heard this.

Hindsight: I am intervening prematurely; it would have been better to formulate a silent hypothesis at this point and to wait for the patient's further thoughts before intervening. I had been selective in my playback of the patient's own words, avoiding any reference to the pool of blood or to there having been a birth and a death in the first dream. The patient now offers a second dream, in which she was swimming in a pool. We cannot be sure whether this is a confirmation of the interpretation offered, as I am assuming in the session, or whether it is an indication by the patient that I have been going too fast. She again gives no associations, as if to highlight the fact that I had interpreted the earlier dream almost on my own. I had responded too quickly and with few associations from her.

> I said I thought this second dream stressed her need to go at her own pace. She replied that she was actually 'crawling' (doing the crawl) in the dream, and she added that Peter was now experimenting with crawling.

Internal supervision: I feel these comments are further confirmation of my interpretation that she needed to go at her own pace.

Hindsight: I am too quick to hear confirmation of this interpretation. The concern about the flexible arrangement is not being confronted directly in this session, and I fail to notice the omission. I am still assuming this flexibility to be what the patient needs, so I am deaf to any indications to the contrary.

> Mrs B. then told me she wanted to explore the question of the Friday sessions further. I suggested to her she could do

one of two things, with regard to Fridays: either she could use her Friday time on a demand-feeding basis, asking for the extra session during those weeks when she felt a need for it, or she could go back to five sessions for as long as needed. I suggested she let me know which way she would like to arrange the Friday sessions when she felt ready to decide.

Hindsight: There has been a further shift away from an analytic approach to the unresolved problem of the Friday sessions. Instead, alternate arrangements are being suggested to her. We also need to note that I have shifted into a manipulative mode. I am directive, making suggestions, and offering solutions to the patient rather than allowing her to be free to find her own. By intervening prematurely, I cut across the patient saying whatever she had just started to say, deflecting her onto the alternative arrangements I am now suggesting to her.

Towards the end of this session, I introduced a new topic, saying I felt it might be related to the matter at hand but I was not certain. I wondered aloud to the patient whether she had needed to emphasize the importance for her of being allowed to go at her own pace. She had, for instance, made sure she did not direct my attention from the baby part of herself either by bringing her actual baby to show me or by bringing a photograph of him.

Hindsight: The possibility that there might be some significance in Mrs B.'s never having volunteered to bring her baby to a session had been suggested to me some months earlier, when I had attended a clinical presentation by a female analyst who was talking specifically about her experience with patients who had been pregnant during analysis. She had quoted several such cases, in all of which the mother had at some stage brought the baby to a session. When I mentioned I had a patient who had never brought her baby to a session, the patient having been pregnant while in analysis with me, I was told that I may have been blocking her from feeling able to show me her baby; perhaps I had been communicating some jealousy of her relationship with her baby, from which I was excluded. I had not thought so at the time, and I had felt no need to bring this issue up with her until now. For some reason I chose to mention this now, even though it was manifestly quite irrelevant and far removed from the issues that were much more in evidence in this session.

I am still blocking the analytic process by remaining in a manipulative mode of functioning. I say I am not sure whether this new topic relates to the matter at hand. My introduction of this here suggests some unrecognized need (of mine) to direct the patient away from what is disturbing the present state of the analytic relationship. Indications of countertransference are present in the manipulative quality of my intervention and in the implied pressure upon the patient to feel that she 'should' bring her baby, or a photograph of him, to show me.

> Mrs B. replied to this by saying she hadn't felt I needed to see the baby, or a photograph of him, because she had assumed I already knew him so well through her. (This was the end of the session.)

Internal supervision: I feel reprimanded by the patient. In her response she points out that I should not need to see her baby, or a photograph of him, at least not for the purposes of the analysis. She indicates that she had assumed I knew him well through her, but now she may be wondering whether I do. Her use of the word 'need' alerts me to the fact that she is picking up some countertransference interest expressed by me. However, because it is the end of the session, this is not dealt with. Having allowed my internal supervision to lapse in this session, I shall have to be more alert in the future. The unresolved issues are likely to appear as a continuing concern in the next session(s).

Tuesday

The patient arrived six minutes late. This was most unusual for her. She started the session standing, and offered two photographs to me while I was also still standing.

Internal supervision: The patient prompts me to see that there is something amiss, by coming unusually late. She also demonstrates, by standing, that the photographs do not belong in the analysis.

Hindsight: We can see a silent protest here along with the patient's compliance, but I fail to use my awareness of this in the current session.

> One photograph was of Mrs B. with her baby when he was a few weeks old, and the other was a more recent photograph of him with both parents. I responded to these by saying 'They are lovely', and handed the photos back to her. She lay down on the couch.
>
> After a pause, Mrs B. repeated what she had said at the end of the previous day's session, that she had felt I already knew her baby and her husband intimately without seeing the photographs; but, outwardly, she seemed pleased I had seen what they look like.

Hindsight: We can note her repetition that I should not have needed to see the photographs. Even though initially I had been alert to this as a break in the normal analytic boundary I fail to deal with it in this session, possibly because there are now several framework issues to be dealt with.

> The patient continued by saying she was still not sure about the fifth sessions. She didn't know whether it should be on a demand-feeding basis or not, as she might end up wanting her session on every Friday.

Internal supervision: This question of the flexible arrangement remains unresolved, and the patient continues to be anxious about it. The idea of demand-feeding had been introduced by me, not by her. The effect of this is to make her feel she would be greedy if she were to ask for a full return to five sessions per week.

Mrs B. went on to say she didn't want me to assume too many of the Friday times would be available to me for my reading.

Internal supervision: More errors come home to roost. Mrs B. specifically picks up the unconscious implications of my earlier self-exposure with regard to the reading. She shows here quite clearly how she is reacting to these implications; that she is anxious I might want the Friday time *for me* when she could be needing this same time for herself. The offer of a demand-feeding arrangement is not turning out to be as reassuring as it was meant to be. It is making the patient feel criticized, as being 'demanding' if she should need her Friday time back. In the guise of seeming to be generous to the patient over the Friday times, I have projected some unacknowledged greedi-ness of my own into the patient.

I said I felt it had been unhelpful telling her how I planned to use her time, while keeping it available to her. Knowing this, she now saw me as the mother who wanted to be allowed to get on with her own things once the child was beginning to grow up. I was aware of the implications of this for her, because her accident had occurred at a time when her mother was busy elsewhere – and at that time she herself had just recently begun to walk.

Hindsight: There is an attempt here to acknowledge the patient's reality perception before referring to any childhood precedent to it. But, I am still being too quick to pass on to the past from the uncomfortable reality in the present. In effect, I am deflecting the patient away from my own failure in attention to that of her mother. This could be seen by her as a further indication of my sense of discomfort at the recent lapses in the analysis. I do not leave her free to elaborate on this, in her own way or in her own time. I pre-empt her by doing this for her.

Mrs B. replied to this by remembering in some detail how her mother always seemed to be putting housework and cooking before spending time with the children. Her mother always wanted to have the house cleaned, and a good meal prepared, as if all they needed was to be housed and fed, whereas Mrs B. would have preferred a simple lunch and more time with her mother.

Internal supervision: The patient seems to be playing back her perception of me as having been preoccupied with getting the recent mess in the analysis cleaned up, and myself reinstated as the good mother ready with a good meal, whereas she would have preferred me to have allowed her to have had more time in the session for her to have used this in her own way.

Mrs B. went on to tell me about about her nephew (aged nine) and niece (aged seven) who were staying with them at this time. Her niece had been away for the weekend. She had a favourite cookery book that she had brought with her for her stay; and she had also taken this with her for the weekend, so her brother would not use it while she was away. Mrs B. had let her nephew use one of her own recipes for him to cook with her, which he wanted to do. Half way through making something in the kitchen with her, he complained that she was not really letting him do the cooking. She was doing too much of it for him.

Internal supervision: I regard this as unconscious supervision by the patient. I reflect on this and feel she is alerting me to my having done too much for her, in her recent sessions, in relation either to the frequency of the sessions or to the issue of the photographs or both. I prepare to explore each of these in turn.

Hindsight: What I do not recognize here is the theme of *two people wanting the same thing*. The niece wants to keep her cookery book for herself, to prevent her brother using it when she is away. The patient may be alluding to my telling her I would use her time on Fridays for myself when she is away. She could feel I am wanting the time for myself, not wanting her to have it.

I said I felt she needed to confirm that she was being allowed enough freedom for her decision about the Friday sessions to be really her own. Mrs B. replied to this by saying she didn't feel I was interfering in any way with that. There was then a silence.

Internal supervision: I note the word 'interfering', and again I feel rebuked by the patient. I sense this might be related more directly to the photographs.

I said to Mrs B. I felt perhaps the missing freedom had more to do with the fact that I, and not she, had raised the issue of the photographs. Although she had complied with my comments, apparently happily, I felt she may have had more reservations about doing so than she had been showing. She picked this up quite readily and said that, although she was pleased I had seen the photographs, she was aware of being anxious I might assume from them that everything was now all right. Everyone looked so well and happy in the photos. She was afraid I might be unaware that, inside herself, she was still having to deal with more distress than she felt able to cope with in four sessions per week.

Internal supervision: I note the patient is elaborating on her anxiety related to showing me the photos, and she inserts a further reference to the still unresolved question of frequency. I see that I must attend to this now.

I said she was clearly still anxious about the question of the Friday sessions. She replied that she was, and asked if she could (at least) come this week on the Friday. This was agreed to.

Hindsight: The issue of the treatment structure is only partly resolved. It was not until after this week that Mrs B. made an unreserved request for a return to five times per week, on a regular basis, which was how the analysis continued.

Mrs B. continued by telling me a dream:
She was holding a container with something valuable in it. There were other people around and they seemed to want

> *their share of what was in the container. She felt as if they*
> *had robbed a bank, or something, and she was now*
> *carrying the loot for all of them. They were sent to prison,*
> *but there was a friendly prison officer who saw to it that she*
> *was put into a cell on her own for her protection. She*
> *finished her sentence before the others. She was being*
> *conducted across the yard towards the gate to freedom*
> *when the others set upon her and kicked her head in. She*
> *lay dead on the ground.* Mrs B.'s subsequent associations
> referred to the analysis, but I could not recall these after the
> session had ended.

Internal supervision: I feel flooded by this dream and the
associations. I am abstracting the themes in the dream while
listening to what the patient is saying. I choose to play back
those themes I can recognize as relating to the analysis, and to
the current issues regarding it.

Hindsight: There is a further reference to the theme of *other
people wanting what she has,* what she is holding in the container,
but I miss this and therefore still do not deal with the issue of
the Friday time being no longer clearly hers. Also, my not
being able to recall the patient's associations indicates a
difficulty in following, rather than leading, her in this session.

> I said the patient was trying to preserve her analysis, as the
> container with something valuable in it, from whatever was
> threatening to take it from her. She needed me to be a
> protector of it, allowing her to have space to herself,
> particularly as she may have felt I intruded on her space by
> my reference to her bringing her baby or a photograph of
> him. Maybe she saw me as being jealous of her special
> relationship with her baby, wanting some of it for me too.

Hindsight: This attempt at interpretation is too long. Also I
refer ambiguously to two kinds of intrusion by me: (1) into the
analytic space, and (2) into her space with her baby. The
reference to jealousy is a further carry-over from the comments made by my senior colleague about babies born during
an analysis.

Mrs B. agreed with what I had said (an agreement too easy to be convincing) and added that she thought her reason for not bringing her baby to show me was that she wanted to be allowed to have something all to herself.

Internal supervision: She picks up what makes most sense to her from what I have been saying, and she adopts the same ambiguity in her response 'something all to herself', as I had used. This phrase can refer either to the analytic relationship which she does not want shared with any third party, or to her relationship with her baby which she does not want me to intrude on. I choose to pick up first the matter of the analytic frame.

I replied that this comment is particularly true of her wish to have her analysis to herself, without having other people intrude upon her being allowed to use her sessions in her own way.

Hindsight: I have stopped hiding behind the ambiguity and have acknowledged that the analytic frame requires privacy, not being subjected to suggestion or directives from the analyst. Had I responded to the earlier cues, with regard to the Friday time, I could have been more specific here. She is also wanting the Friday time to be 'all to herself'.

She said that this was true, and she began to relax in the session for the first time, having been noticeably tense. She remained calm until the end of the session, a few minutes later, without talking.

Internal supervision: During the silence I begin to realize that the attack upon the patient, in the dream, has not been referred to by me or by her. I have selected only those themes in which I can see myself reflected in a positive light. Because I have ducked the negative references, she could see me as not yet ready to tolerate the more painful perceptions of me.

Wednesday

Mrs B. arrived eight minutes late. Still standing (again), before moving to the couch, she asked me if she had left the smaller photograph anywhere in my room the previous day. I told her I had not seen it.

Internal supervision: She is using the same defence of isolation as before (i.e. standing rather than using the couch). She is also late again. I recognize that something is still interfering with the analytic space.

> Mrs B. told me she was late because the car wouldn't start. 'There was no light in the battery', and it was only the second time that this had happened with this car. She had then taken her husband's car. She hadn't looked in her own car for the missing photo.

Internal supervision: I hear of something that has been lost, something to do with her having brought the photographs the previous day. I listen to this, around the current framework issue related to the photos. I try to find a bridge towards dealing with this.

Hindsight: 'No light in the battery' is a strange way of referring to a flat battery. English is not the patient's original language, but as she is fluent this expression stands out as unusual for her. There may be a reference to my not having been more enlightened in my recent handling of her sessions. I have become like the car – not working properly.

> I said she may have needed to feel that the photo had been lost, for the purpose of this session, so we could look at the implications of this for her. For instance, she could feel (with some justification) that she would not have lost this photo if I hadn't mentioned she might show it to me. She agreed. She then wanted to refer back to the previous day's dream.

Internal supervision: Again her agreement is too quick. I am left feeling unsure whether this is confirmation. I note, however, the patient's indication that there is something we have not looked at left over from the previous day's dream.

Mrs B. pointed out to me her passivity in relation to the people threatening her in the dream. She saw them as people from her past. She commented that she could not gain anything if she merely sought protection from them rather than facing them.

Internal supervision: The patient picks up one of the aspects of the dream I had bypassed in my selective play-back of themes from the dream. She also offers a deflection from me onto people from her past. She may have registered that I had previously avoided the negative references to me in the dream. I think she could be expressing a perception of me as needing to be protected from her more negative feelings. I also note her passivity in relation to my comment about the photographs.

Hindsight: We can see how the patient parallels my own defensive manoeuvre in the previous session, when I deflected her too quickly from my own failure onto the failure of her mother. This could be seen as a further indication to her that I might have been feeling unable to cope with the critical allusions to me in her dream.

I said it seemed to me that I appeared in two forms in her dream: as the prison officer, who is seen as friendly and who is putting her into protective custody, and I might also be represented in the dream by the people threatening her.

Internal supervision: This is a clumsy attempt to bring the patient back to the present reality, rather than collude with a possible flight to the past.

Hindsight: I am interpreting without giving the patient time to present me with the material for an interpretation. I am therefore still acting upon my countertransference anxiety at having made so many mistakes recently, one leading to another.

> Mrs B. seemed puzzled by the second part of my inter-
> pretation and asked me how I had arrived at it.

Internal supervision: The patient points out that I have picked
my interpretation out of thin air. Certainly, she has not given
me the grounds for this intervention, in the course of this
session, so naturally she cannot see where I have got it from. I
am in too much hurry to correct my recent errors. I therefore
try to remedy this situation by playing back some of the
missing ingredients from the dream, hoping to provide a
bridge from that to my interpretation.

Hindsight: It would have been better to remain silent and let
the patient lead.

> I said I felt we should see how the dream had started. She
> had been carrying something valuable in a container,
> which she was trying to protect from the other people in the
> dream who were seen as wanting to have their share of it.
> She had also told me she had had some reluctance about
> showing me her baby. Nevertheless, she had brought the
> photos and she had had this dream the following night. At
> the end of the dream her head is kicked in, possibly a
> reference to her feeling she had not been allowed to think
> for herself. She reflected on this and partly agreed with it.
> She added that she hadn't been conscious of any wish not to
> bring the photographs; it had merely not crossed her mind
> to do so.

Internal supervision: I note that it had 'not crossed her mind', in
other words it was not her own thinking. I see this as some
degree of confirmation, and I feel that perhaps we can now
look at the transference elaboration of this experience.

Hindsight: It is evident I remain impatient to move away from
the present reality. By not giving her time to continue from
here on her own, I am still threatening her space while
acknowledging her need for me not to do so.

> I said it was possible I had come to represent a bit of her
> past experience with her mother, in which she had not felt

able to stand up to her, or in this instance to me. Instead, it appeared that she had felt a need to please me by bringing the photographs; but this apparent need may have been caused by her seeing me, at the time, as the mother who needed to be pleased. Mrs B. was nodding as I was making the last part of this interpretation. She went on to tell me about something that happened 'on Friday – no, Thursday night' of the previous week.

Internal supervision: The slip seems obvious. I see this as a reference to the missing Friday sessions.

Hindsight: The Friday issue is dealt with only temporarily here. It is not until after this week that the Friday sessions are reinstated on a regular basis, so in this sense the Fridays are still missing.

Mrs B. continued by saying that on Thursday evening her husband had been away, so she had invited herself to supper with friends. She told me in detail about a rich sweet dish that she took with her to the supper, how she had eaten too much and had then felt sick. In the night she had been afraid she might be ill the following day and unable to feed Peter, who was still being breast-fed. She therefore made herself vomit; and by the morning she was feeling better and more able to cope.

Internal supervision: I note the themes: husband absent; feeding herself; making herself feel sick by eating too much; fear of having to interrupt her baby's feeding. I decide to offer a bridge towards dealing with some of this.

I pointed out to Mrs B. the timing of this experience, prior to the Friday morning when she would not be having her usual session. She agreed it was probably because she was feeling deprived of the Friday session that she had allowed herself to eat too much.

Internal supervision: She gets to this on her own. I do not need to over-feed her.

> She also pointed out that she was aware of having had a choice: either to remain feeling ill and helpless, or to do something about it in order not to have to interrupt her present feeding pattern with her baby.

Internal supervision: She indicates the theme of interruption, which I see as alluding to interruptions of various kinds. I decide not to interrupt here.

> She went on to say it would not necessarily have meant having to wean Peter abruptly; but certainly she thought it would have meant an unwarranted interruption of the feeding pattern.

Internal supervision: I note the words 'unwarranted interruption'. The issue I feel she is highlighting, with her reference to feeding, is that of the Friday sessions – one of which was the previous Friday just referred to.

> I said to her she had come to experience the recent interruption of her Friday sessions as unwarranted. On the Monday, in her first session after the sequence she had just described, she had indicated that she wanted to review the decision to drop Friday sessions. She agreed. It was by this time the end of the session.

Internal supervision: I think it only became possible for Mrs B. to refer to the dropping of her Friday sessions as an unwarranted interruption once it had been agreed that she could come back to her Friday session, at least for this week. The long-term arrangement has still not been settled.

Thursday

Mrs B. started the session by telling me about Emma's mother. This mother had said that Emma should stay the night with Mrs B. and her niece. She had also said in front of

Emma: 'It would be so nice for me.' Mrs B. felt terrible about this, feeling very sorry for the child and feeling she should have been given a chance to say what *she* wanted. Mrs B. went on to say it seemed wrong to push Emma out of her own home in this way, to please her mother.

Internal supervision: I seem to be hearing about a self-interested mother. Listening first for the external realities being alluded to here, I wondered if that incident were being told to me as a further unconscious prompt from the patient. I decide to start with this as a bridge-comment towards exploring the patient's internal reality, which I believe is being indirectly referred to here.

I said to Mrs B. that here we have an example of a child being separated from her mother, because of wishes of the mother rather than of the child, and the child had not been given a chance to say what she felt about it. Mrs B. agreed and fell into a distressed silence. After a while she told me that, during the previous night, she had awakened thinking she heard a child calling 'Mummy'. The older children were both soundly asleep. She went to see Peter but realized (of course) he could not talk yet. She then noticed that the voice had been saying 'Mummee', which was how a child would call for a mother in her own childhood language. She relapsed into silence and was noticeably more distressed.

Internal supervision: There is ample confirmation here of the theme of an *absent mother*. I feel she needs some acknowledgement by me, that I am aware of the meaning of her distress, rather than having me leave her too long in a silence in which I also could be seen as the mother who cannot hear.

I said: 'So it was the child in you calling out for your childhood mother.' She agreed and heaved a sigh of relief. She added that she could not count on her mother to hear. She went on to ask why it was she still went on and on with the same problems, and again became silent.

Internal supervision: I reflect that the patient is needing help to deal with feelings about her absent mother, and I feel she is also alerting me to my recent absences (my lapses of analytic attention), which triggered this material. I look for a current focus to this theme of inattention, where I could have been failing her in ways like the mothers she is criticizing (Emma's mother and her own).

> After a fairly long silence, I said that what set this off again in her might have been her uncertainty about whether I had been offering her flexibility, with regard to the sessions, to meet *her* needs or whether I was really wanting to get on with my own business. (I was silently bearing in mind that I had told her I would be using her time for myself.) Mrs B. said that consciously she had been glad I had explained to her about the reading.

Internal supervision: I note her emphasis on 'consciously', so I wonder about the unconscious aspect.

> I said I felt that to her unconscious, my having told her about my wish to have time for reading had given her occasion to develop a perception of me as being too much like her mother, wanting to have time to get on with her own things, and like Emma's mother who had behaved in a similar way. Mrs B. said the child part of her would probably latch onto anything like that to feel anxious about. She said she was wondering whether her need to go back to five times per week had stemmed from a need to be sure that her Friday times would still really be there for her.

Internal supervision: I see some of this as a confirmatory response, but I find myself wondering about the original dropping of the Friday sessions, whether the arrangement had been such as to allow this to happen too readily.

> I said I felt perhaps she had become unsure where she stood with me, once I had offered to let the structure of her sessions become flexible. She might have accepted this change partly because it had been made to appear

seductively easy rather than her having been given a chance to work this through, to have her own say on it, to the point of being sufficiently clear in herself to take this step on her own.

Internal supervision: I am beginning to get hold of the point I had missed until now; it could have been the *flexibility* that had made things so difficult for the patient. The analytic framework had begun to suffer further breaks from that point on.

Mrs B. replied she didn't know about this; but shortly afterwards she said that she had suddenly developed a splitting headache, and she said it was most unlike her to have headaches.

Internal supervision: She is telling me there is still a painful conflict around here. I listen for further cues.

After a silence, Mrs B. began to tell me about feeding Peter. He had a great appetite and at this time happily ate solids during the day, but he continued to be breast-fed in the mornings and the evenings. Until recently she had felt she needed to be very careful about what she herself ate, in order to be sure she had an adequate supply of milk and a proper balance in her milk for the baby. She had since discovered that she really didn't need to be so 'ultra careful', and her baby had continued to be perfectly all right.

Internal supervision: I hear further unconscious prompting here. I have been too careful with Mrs B., in thinking she needs flexibility; so my attempts to hold her particularly carefully around the time of 'weaning' in the analysis have made her more anxious and insecure, not less so. As a result, I have lost my balance as analyst and I am still in the process of having to recover this.

I said perhaps she had experienced me as being overly careful with her, offering her such a gradual change from

five-times-per-week to four-times, that she felt I was
thinking of her as more fragile in this respect than she
actually was. Mrs B. replied with surprise saying her
headache had gone now.

Internal supervision: I take this as confirmation of my interpretation, and so does she. I then reflect upon this theme of my
trying to be the over-protective mother, in preparation for my
next interpretation.

I said there had been a painful conflict in her. She had been
anxious for me to be sensitive to her child needs, in order
that my behaviour did not appear too similar to the
insensitivities she had experienced in her mother; but she
also needed me to acknowledge her adult strengths. She
agreed that she would feel I was letting her down either
way: if I responded only to the child in her or only to the
adult.

As the session was ending, and she was about to leave, the
patient added that she wondered whether she had pointed
out to me she still had the negative of the lost photograph.
She had noted to herself that still having the negative meant
she could re-create the positive. I said I felt she had needed
me to learn from her, in order to recognize what had been a
negative experience in the past few sessions, so we could
re-establish the positive which had been lost. She nodded
and smiled her agreement as she left.

Internal supervision: The analytic holding seems to have been
recovered. The patient has found her own symbolic way of
letting me know this.

Comment: It should be noted that my preoccupation with the
recent mistakes (although necessary as a step towards resuming the analytic process) was also presenting a degree of
interference. This concern over errors is always a hazard if the
work of the internal supervisor is allowed to become too active
and conscious during a session. It then functions instead as an
internalized supervisor, which at times can even become

persecutory to the therapist. (This is especially true if the clinical material in question is going to be presented to scrutiny by others, as in a clinical seminar, which was the case here.)

My recent high level of concern is being pointed out by the patient as being 'ultra careful'. I had been giving her a pain in the head. Even though I do not recognize this particular contribution to her headache, in the current session, her headache lifts when I show that I acknowledge there had been too much carefulness somewhere and, by implication, that I am ready to relax and to allow the analytic process to be resumed.

Friday

The patient arrived slightly late. She referred to the previous Wednesday night, when she had had a dream she had forgotten until that morning.

Internal supervision: The patient had 'forgotten' this dream. Maybe she could not let herself remember it while we were still caught up in other matters. She is also late, so there may be something still holding her back.

In the dream *there was a river. She was lying beside this river, the sides of which were like springtime with new growth all around. She was either very small or was lying on her front as the water seemed to be at eye-level. It had then begun boiling and threatened to destroy everything around. She felt the boiling water was coming straight at her. She wanted to turn away, because she was so frightened, but instead she looked at the water and it became an ordinary river again.* The patient paused in her recounting of the dream and said with amazement: 'I was able to stop it boiling.'

Internal supervision: I note the themes in this dream: spring-time and new growth; the patient is very small or lying on her front; there is eye-level water; the water begins to boil; it threatens to destroy; it seems to be coming straight at her. I sense that I am being presented with a traumatic memory, or a

dream-reconstruction, of the accident. The boiling water had
been at eye-level, and it was the patient's front that had been so
badly burned. She also seems to indicate a readiness to look at
the water. Possibly she is letting me know that the 'memory',
which had always been too terrible to remember, is close to
being consciously re-called. Just possibly she is feeling more
secure now we have worked all week on re-establishing the
analytic framework. I decide to explore this with her, but
being careful not to lead her towards my own thoughts about
the dream. She needs to be ready to see the implications of this
for herself.

> I commented that the river had stopped boiling once she
> was able to look at it. I also noted she had 'forgotten' this
> dream until she felt safe enough with me to look at it. She
> replied she hadn't realized until telling me the dream that it
> so clearly referred to the accident. She then became very
> distressed and began to experience the accident as
> happening to her in the session. It was as if the boiling water
> were pouring onto her and burning her. She cried out
> loudly in extreme pain and sat up, saying: 'When I was lying
> down it wouldn't stop coming at me.' She sobbed for a long
> time, holding her head in her hands.

Internal supervision: Her holding of her head in her hands
prompts me to see that she needs to feel held. I recall that
earlier in the analysis she had told me that, after the accident,
the pain only ever felt tolerable when she was being carried by
her mother. She had felt as if she had been able to 'put' her
pain into her mother; but when her mother laid her down
again it had been as if the pain were too much for her mother,
so it seemed as if she were 'putting it back' into the patient.

I cannot but feel under enormous stress, being with the
patient now in this session. It is excruciating. I feel a very
powerful wish to stop this experience, in any way possible, by
trying to reassure her or by trying to divert her: anything
seems preferable to remaining witness to her pain. Alongside
this impulse to protect myself is a realization that this had been
Mrs B.'s perception of her mother's response. For the patient's

sake, therefore, I know I must find some way of staying with her through what is happening, without trying to by-pass it.

> I said I felt she was holding her own head in her hands as a way of telling me that she needed to feel 'held' through this experience. Still crying, she replied: 'My mother couldn't face it – she had to turn away from it – I couldn't bear it alone.'

Internal supervision: I recall that her mother had in effect caused the accident by not being in the room, where this now mobile child was and where there was water boiling. After the accident her mother had not been able to look at the results of the accident. Mrs B. had a memory image of her mother dressing the wounds while trying to turn her face away from them. I feel I am being tested by the patient to see if I can bear to see her in such pain. She is telling me she cannot bear this alone.

> I said to her: 'You need me to be able to stay with you in your pain and not to have to turn away from it.' She looked me straight in the eyes (she was still sitting on the couch) and said: 'Can you?' I answered: 'I know you need me to bear it with you.' After this she lay down, saying: 'Let me see if it has stopped now. Before, the boiling water kept coming at me. I could not bear the pain. It is better now.' After a while she added: 'I never believed I could bear to remember it; but now I have.'

Internal supervision: This is a quite different level of experience from all the earlier allusions to the accident. Mrs B. had dreamed of the accident a number of times, but it was always more disguised. For instance, the boiling water had often been represented by its opposite, by ice. In one dream it was the movement of the water that was frozen, as it began to fall towards her like in a photograph. I note the progression.

> I said to Mrs B. that this was the first time she had let herself experience the accident undisguised. She replied: 'This

time I let it flow over me; and, even though it burned me, I
now find that I am all right.' At the end of the session she
again looked straight at me and said: 'Thank you for staying
with me.'

Aftermath of the sequence

The following week Mrs B. told me she had realized that she
had been singing to herself over the weekend. This was
something quite new, and it reminded her of her mother
singing to her. She recalled prodding her mother to get her to
go on singing when she stopped. This was the first remembered link between a good mother from before the accident
and a good mother still there after it.

What followed later was the patient's hating me most
intensely, as the mother who had allowed the accident to
happen to her and as the analyst who had allowed it to be
repeated in the analysis. She also had to test me out extensively
to discover whether I could continue to hold her analytically.
She expected me to become the mother who could not bear
remaining in touch with her pain, or who might retaliate if
being in touch with this became unbearable to me. She
expected to be left to fall for ever. (Part of that sequence is
described in Chapter Seven.)

It took a further year before Mrs B. could begin to find real
peace from the unspeakable dread of the anxieties which had
come to be so closely associated with her experience of intense
dependence on her mother after the accident, and on me as
analyst after she had re-experienced the accident in the
analysis. Much else, of course, occurred during the next year
of treatment, but the experience of the week reported here
remained a basic foundation to most of the subsequent
progress made in the analysis.

Discussion

The interactional viewpoint

As in Chapter Three, this presentation illustrates a number of
points that are most clearly observed when the clinical
sequence is considered from an interactional viewpoint.

It shows once again how closely a patient monitors the analyst. Mrs B. not only noted my conscious interventions, and other expressions of myself, but she also monitored for the unconscious implications of my behaviour; my intrusions, my deflections, my timing of interventions or failures to inter-vene, my choice of what I referred to and what I had overlooked, and my capacity to cope with what she needed to be able to present to me or my unreadiness for this.

Also, by a series of cues offered to me, this patient was able to help considerably in the re-establishing of a more secure analytic framework – without which she could not have re-experienced in the analysis the memory which she had felt she might not survive remembering.

Evidence of indirect countertransference

One influence affecting this week's work with Mrs B. was my knowing that I had decided to present it to a clinical seminar, at which a number of senior colleagues would be present. The seminar leader was also known to be rigorous in his criticism.

Having chosen to present whatever happened in this week, with this particular patient, my listening was already less relaxed than I would wish. The work of my internal super-vision became tilted away from the more sublimal way of working I wish to advocate, and at times it was more like that of a severe internalized supervisor. I was internalizing the anticipated critical attitude of the seminar leader – 'identifying with the aggressor'. This intrusive presence of an influence from outside the analytic situation is what has been described as 'indirect countertransference' (Racker 1968). To that extent, therefore, this work is not an illustration of how a more autonomous and relaxed process of internal supervision should be.

Countertransference and role-responsiveness

There is also evidence that I was responding to the patient with personal countertransference.

At some level, I must have known there was more to be dealt with in this (so far) quite short analysis. Mrs B's accident had been analytically encountered at various levels, all of them significantly less traumatic than the accident itself. The patient had dreamed about this many times, always with a high degree of 'dream-work' disguise (Freud 1900:461n). But it had never been experienced in the session. I had assumed that so early a trauma could not be really remembered or re-lived in an analysis. I now recognize I must have hoped this, so that I would not have to be confronted by the impact of this trauma upon myself.

With hindsight, it is also possible to recognize there was a likelihood Mrs B. would become anxious at the time when she began to feel better because it had been when she was beginning to be a normal lively toddler, exploring the world around her, that the accident had occurred.[2] So, when she felt better and suggested she might be ready to drop one of her sessions, I should have been more alert to the possible significance of this for her. However, it must have suited me unconsciously to collude with the patient's confidence, I too wishing to think we had been through the worst of her analysis already.

When Mrs B. became anxious, immediately she had begun to do without her fifth session, I was getting early warning signals that all was not as well as it had appeared.

When I introduced the topic of her baby, that she had not brought him or a photograph of him to show me, this looks (at first sight) entirely unaccountable. On reflection, however, it begins to make more sense if we see this in terms of what it did to the analysis. It temporarily deflected the analysis onto the patient's *well baby*, and away from the *unwell baby* in her unconscious memory. She later pointed this out, when she explained her reservations about my seeing how well she looked in the photographs; that I might assume everything to be all right, and I might therefore overlook that there were very difficult things still to be dealt with.

In the process of this accumulation of errors, there began to be an uncanny parallel between how I was behaving with this patient and how her mother had been at the time of the accident. I was too quick to assume her readiness to cope more on her own, when she first said she was feeling much better. I agreed to drop the fifth session without a careful analysis of the implications. I compounded this by telling her how I would be using her time, that I would be using it for my own business. So, by these several stages, I came to represent her mother who had been prematurely absent from her child at the time when she was at risk as a toddler needing more active attention rather than less.

Can this parallel be explained only in terms of personal countertransference? I think there must have been some unconscious role-responsiveness too, which contributed to my becoming so fully involved in this re-enactment of the mother who had failed this patient at the time of the original trauma.

The recovery of analytic holding

This patient could not dare to experience her original trauma while the state of the analytic framework and holding continued to be inadequate and therefore insecure.

An essential part of this sequence, in my opinion, emerges through the patient's tenacious cueing of me to see those things that were still not right. By listening to the sequence interactionally, and by gradually recognizing and attending to her anxiety concerning whether I could bear to stay with her pain in the analysis (rather than to divert her), she rediscovered that I could be responsive to her cues. The analytic hold thus came to be restored; and the patient was able to acknowledge this symbolically in the Thursday session.

Re-experiencing the original trauma

Before this week of analysis, I was not familiar with Winnicott's notion that the details from early traumatic events are 'catalogued' (Winnicott 1958:247). Elsewhere, in his paper 'Mind and its Relation to the Psycho-Soma', he writes:

> 'One has to include in one's theory of the development of a human being the idea that it is normal and healthy for the individual to be able to defend the self against specific environmental failure by a *freezing of the failure situation*. Along with this goes an unconscious assumption (which can become a conscious hope) that opportunity will occur at a later date for a renewed experience in which the failure situation will be able to be unfrozen and re-experienced, with the individual in a regressed state, in an environment that is making adequate adaptation.'
> (Winnicott 1958:281)

Mrs B. unconsciously found her own way back to the moment of trauma, by degrees which were in proportion to her fragile but growing trust in my capacity to hold her through these experiences. Earlier in the analysis she had only been able to enumerate the details as they had been told to her. Later she could let herself dream about them.[3] She needed eventually to experience, in the transference, the 'unthinkable anxieties' of her childhood and in particular the 'fear of falling' (Winnicott 1965b:58, 1970).

The analysis gradually moved towards a situation which, in important respects, replicated the earlier experience of failure. Gradually, too, she helped me to represent 'an environment that is making adequate adaptation' Only then could she combine in her analysis a representation of the original failure with an unconscious hope that (this time) she could go through the experience in the presence of someone able to stay with her through it, with herself and the other person both able to survive that intensity of feeling.

Here again, as in example 4.6, 'the patient uses the analyst's failures, often quite small ones, perhaps manoeuvred by the patient'. The patient was then able to use me to represent the mother who had previously failed her. The 'failure situation' had become unfrozen, and she could now attack me with the feelings she had first experienced towards her mother, at the time of the accident (Winnicott 1965b:258). If these dynamics do apply here too, it is remarkable how precisely the details of the original failure were unwittingly repeated in this analysis.

I had to learn how to survive these attacks. What helped most in this was my being able to recognize the unconscious purpose in this sequence, and the cost to the patient if I were to collapse or retaliate.

Notes

1. The clinical sequence presented in this chapter is an extract from my paper 'The Reflective Potential of the Patient as Mirror to the Therapist'. In James O. Raney (ed) (1984) *Listening and Interpreting: The Challenge of the Work of Robert Langs.* New York: Jason Aronson.

2. I have noticed, with a number of patients, that the experience of *feeling better* is sometimes treated by the patient as a signal for further

anxiety. Some analysts might treat this as a fear of losing the 'secondary gains from illness'. Others might regard it as 'negative therapeutic reaction'. However, I believe there are some occasions when a patient is indicating that an unconscious link has been formed between an earlier experience of trauma and the prior sense of safety, as if that 'safety' had been a warning signal for the pending disaster. Perhaps an unconscious set is formed in which feeling safe and subsequent catastrophe are seen as forever linked.

3. Winnicott says: 'That which has been dreamed and remembered and presented is within the capacity of the ego-strength and structure' (Winnicott 1965:254).

6

Key dynamics of containment

By using internal supervision, and trial identification in particular, I shall examine some failures to contain. We can then see more clearly the dynamics that are involved in what I am here calling 'containment'. I shall also illustrate how insight and analytic holding are helped by an awareness of communication by impact as described in Chapter Four.

Containing

There are times when people cannot cope with their own feelings without some assistance. We could then think of these feelings as spilling over towards others. The analytic view on this phenomenon is to recognize this spilling over, or inability to contain, as an unconscious communication to others that there is something amiss, something that is unmanageable without help.

Basically, the help being searched for is always for *a person* to be available to help with these difficult feelings. Often, however, the response from the people around is to treat those feelings as if they were abnormal or dangerous. Medication can subdue them. Referral elsewhere can alleviate the problem for those otherwise most directly exposed to such pressures; but this seldom changes anything for a patient who inwardly still feels victim to powerful feelings.

If anything, these deflective or suppressive measures can add to the sense that there is an intensity of feeling which nobody could manage. If this were really so then suppression, even by addictive means, might appear to be preferable to continuing with a struggle regarded as having no solution.

I am using the notion of containment here as a general term for the management of another person's difficult feelings, which are otherwise uncontained.[1] There is, of course, a proper place for treatment by medication; and for treatment in hospital, which can offer 'asylum' to those who need a safe place in which to be ill. Nevertheless, it is important to remain aware that it is usually a personal form of containment that is being looked for.

In more human terms, what is needed is a form of holding, such as a mother gives to her distressed child. There are various ways in which one adult can offer to another this holding (or containment). And it can be crucial for a patient to be thus held in order to recover, or to discover maybe for the first time, a capacity for managing life and life's difficulties without continued avoidance or suppression.

When feelings are 'dealt with' through suppression a person can be given a breathing space, during which life's problems may be attended to differently; and for many this is enough to help them through that particular time of stress. This form of help should therefore not be under-valued.

However, there are some people who continue to be gripped by the phantasy that their most difficult feelings can only be dealt with by avoidance. The power to overwhelm, attributed to these unmanageable feelings, is confirmed when others treat them as if they share that assessment of them. It is only when these feelings can be admitted within a relationship that the underlying phantasy can begin to be modified. It is then an altogether different experience (for both patient and therapist) when a patient's attacks upon the therapist are survived knowingly, rather than being deflected because of impervious ignorance. Here it is important that therapists should have insight into what is being re-enacted with them. The survival of the therapist, and the understanding of what is being encountered in this experience, are both central to the patient's ultimate recovery.

I shall first give examples of attempts at reassurance that fail, so that we can see why it is they fail.

Failures to contain

A mis-use of supportive action by the therapist

Example 6.1

A male patient (Mr S.) was seeing me in twice-a-week therapy, coming on Wednesdays and Fridays.

One Friday he had difficulty in speaking. He sounded extremely depressed. After a while, I noticed that there was a sense of foreboding in the way he spoke and in the tone of his presence during the session. I therefore said to him: 'You are not actually referring to suicide, but I am picking up a suicidal feeling in how you are speaking to me to-day.' Mr S. began to cry openly, and agreed that he was finding it extremely difficult to see any future at the moment. He hadn't realized it consciously, but he had been brooding upon suicide. It had been at the back of his mind, but it was definitely there; he had never felt so low.

At this point I misjudged the kind of containment this patient was needing. I found myself thinking about the long break between this Friday session and the next Wednesday. So, I offered to see Mr S. on the Monday, if he would like to have an extra session. He asked me if he could think about this and let me know. I later had a telephone message saying he would be coming for the extra session.

The Monday session began as follows:

Patient: 'I had a dream last night:
I was in a boat, trying to negotiate rapids in a river that was flowing too fast for me to be able to control the boat. There was a man at the back of the boat, helping to steady it. He was actually in the river, steadying the boat with his hands. We got through these rapids to a point where the river became more manageable, and I was able to start rowing again. But the man was still hanging on at the back. Now, instead of helping, he was making it more difficult for me to steer the boat for myself.' (Pause.)

'I have come today because I said I would. In actual fact I am feeling better and I now don't feel this extra session to be necessary; but something happened on Friday that was important. You were able to pick up my suicidal feelings without my having to spell these out to you. That helped me to feel not so completely alone, and it helped me to feel that life was not quite impossible after all.'

Discussion: Mr S. had no hesitation in identifying who the man was, at the back of the boat. He knew that what had helped him most on the Friday had been my awareness of how he was feeling. That had been enough. It was what his mother had not been able to do for him. She had been trapped in her own depression when he was small, still mourning the death of a previous baby.

When I had offered the extra session Mr S. was at first grateful. He later felt obligated – even resentful. It was not what he was needing. This sequence therefore helps to illustrate that trying to reassure, or offering extra support, is often motivated by the helper's own need for reassurance because of the anxiety stirred up by a patient's (or client's) distress. Containment is seldom, if ever, achieved by reassuring the patient.

I had initially been in touch with how Mr S. had been feeling, but my own continuing anxiety led me into being over-active. When I suggested he might come for an extra session, this indicated my doubt that he could find the inner strength he needed. In effect, therefore, I was undermining the strength that he did have. This hindered more than it helped, in his dealing with what lay ahead of him, as if I saw myself as indispensible to his survival. His dream spelled this out with unmistakable clarity.

A mis-use of reassurance

Example 6.2

A therapist was being severely tested by a patient (Miss G.), who was chronically depressed and despairing. (See also Chapter Four, example 4.6.)

Miss G.'s mother had died when she was four. Relatives had failed to provide any adequate replacement home. A children's home had done no better. The patient had come to feel there would never be anybody who could cope with how she was feeling. Everyone had either turned away from her when she cried, as if she were too old still to be crying, or they had sent her away to other relatives and (eventually) to the children's home. She remembered herself as often crying, or trying to hide her crying.

> *Patient:* 'I am afraid you must be beginning to despair of me ever getting better.'
>
> *Therapist:* 'If *I* felt that I would not be here.'

Discussion: When I heard this brief sequence, during a supervision session, I felt a twinge of anxiety through my trial identification with the patient. It brought to my mind what I had already heard about this patient's experience of people who had stopped being there, particularly when she could not stop herself crying. Her despair had been based upon the experience of no-one being prepared to remain in touch with what she was feeling.

I saw the patient's communication as an unconscious prompt, trying to indicate what her testing out of her therapist was about. It seemed possible, indeed likely, that this patient was still in search of someone who could tolerate being in touch with her unbearable despair.

If Miss G. had been looking for this kind of containment, what she heard could have a very different meaning from what was intended. The therapist meant to reassure Miss G. that she was not despairing of being able to help her. But the patient could easily mis-hear this as a confirmation of her dread, that not even her therapist would allow herself to be in touch with her despair and be prepared to go on seeing her: 'If I felt *that* I would not be here.'

The therapist failed to recognize the patient's need to be able to communicate her despair. Had she been more familiar with the unconscious processes operating at the time, she could have tested out her comment before speaking by trial-identifying with the patient. It would have been easier for her to recognize the possibility that Miss G. may have been trying to find out whether her therapist could bear to be in touch with the despair that she herself was feeling.

A principle of interpretation can be drawn from this. Whenever possible, we should interpret what a patient is actually feeling at the time, and not attempt to speak to what we would like the patient to feel instead. Here, Miss G. was feeling despair. A different response could therefore have been along the lines of:

> *Therapist:* 'I believe you are telling me you are afraid that I might not be able to bear being in touch with your despair. Instead you expect that I might in some way stop seeing you, if you were to succeed in communicating your despair to me so that I could actually be feeling it too.'

This form of interpretation would have allowed Miss G. to experience her therapist as really in touch with what she was feeling. Any reassurance to be gained, therefore, could come from being really heard and adequately understood.

When this therapist later overslept (see Chapter Four, example 4.6), that experience took on a terrifying meaning for Miss G. Did it mean her therapist had begun to feel the patient's despair, and was that why she wasn't there? This dramatic enactment of her worst fear required much re-working in the therapy before Miss G. could begin to realize that she had really been able to communicate her despair to her therapist; and (even though it may have contributed to the oversleeping) this had not resulted in an unresolvable collapse, or retaliation, such as the patient had always previously experienced.

Containment by a person

A suicidal patient seen in psychotherapy

Example 6.3

I wish now to give an example of a patient (Mrs F.) who had been regularly dependent upon medication. She had originally turned to this, as a substitute for being 'held' by a person, when she began to find that her life-long self-sufficiency was beginning to crumble. She needed more from a person than anyone seemed able to give her. She therefore became increasingly dependent upon drug substitutes for this. Eventually, she used an overdose of pills in an attempt to kill herself – and (unconsciously) to punish those who had failed to be there for her when she had most needed them.

Mrs F. (aged 50) was referred to me from hospital after a very determined suicide attempt. She had nearly died. This had occurred at a time when she had been feeling acutely anxious, and she had experienced those around her as refusing to be in touch with what she was feeling.

When she started seeing me, there were said to be practical reasons why she could only come once a week. She was still on medication for her anxiety states and insomnia; and she continued to have difficulty in sleeping. Even when she did sleep she would regularly wake to anxiety, which often reached the point of terror.

In one particular session Mrs F. pleaded with me to speak to the referring psychiatrist, to have her medication changed or increased, saying she had to have something to dampen these feelings that were again becoming so unbearable. She was convinced that neither Dr Y. (the referring psychiatrist) nor I had any idea what terrors she was having to go through every day. And nothing was making this any better. She deeply regretted the hospital having succeeded in saving her life.

I agreed to discuss the problem with Dr Y., but I did not promise any change in her medication. I said that I was not convinced it was more pills she was really needing.

> *Patient:* 'You obviously don't understand. Can't you see it is unbearable? You have got to do something. I just cannot go on with these anxieties and terrors, and not sleeping. I NEED MORE PILLS.'
>
> *Therapist:* 'I can see there is something you need more

of. I don't think it is more pills, but what the pills stand for.
I believe there have been times when you needed a
person to be more available to you; but you experienced
that person as unwilling, or unable, to cope with the
intensity of your feelings. So, instead, you have been
trying to shut off those feelings with pills.'

Patient: 'I cannot go on like this. You have got to ask
Dr Y. for more pills, or stronger pills.'

Therapist: 'I will speak to Dr Y.; but I would also like to
suggest that you consider allowing yourself more time
here this week. I could see you in three days' time if you
would be prepared to come then.'

Mrs F. said she would come for the extra session. In the
meantime I spoke to Dr Y., who agreed with me that it
would be a backward step to give into Mrs F.'s demand for
stronger medication. It was clear she was dependent upon
suppressing her feelings, rather than daring to experience
these and to share them with another person in order to
understand them.

Three days later Mrs F. came for her session. She was
calmer and was looking rather embarrassed. She explained what had happened.

After her last session a number of things had emerged. She
had put out her second sleeping pill, to take after midnight
when she still had not got to sleep (which had been her
regular habit). In the morning she had woken to find she
had slept without it.

She then told me about a period in her childhood, when she
had been about three and her mother was busy with her
baby sister. Mrs F. used to go to the local shop, round the
corner from where they lived, and the man behind the
counter used to let her have a dummy. Her mother
objected to her having this and would take it from her; but
the man in the shop used to give her another, whenever she
asked him.

I suggested to Mrs F. that the dummies, which the man used
to give her, stood for her mother whom she was needing but

was having to do without. It seemed that her mother had not responded to the distress signals, which Mrs F. had been giving to her, when she went in search of dummies as her way of telling her mother she needed more time with her. So, when her mother used to remove the dummies without giving her more attention, Mrs F. may have come to feel it was more dummies that she needed. Wanting more pills now was like wanting dummies for the anxious child within herself.

Mrs F. then told me she had been surprised by a memory, during the night when she had slept without the extra sleeping pill: 'It was so vivid it had seemed like a real experience in the present.' She had a sense of being in bed with her mother (which used sometimes to happen when she was small) and feeling her mother's 'big strong back' there beside her. This used to be one of her happiest experiences as a child, being able to be close to her mother while her mother slept.

I said it may have been the only time she felt able to lean upon her mother, to make hidden demands upon her presence while she slept, as there was then no fear of her mother disapproving or turning away from her. Mrs F. agreed, and she began to cry. It then became evident that she found relief from her earlier distress in being able to express this in her crying, in the presence of someone who was prepared to be in touch with what she was feeling.

Discussion: Why was this offer of an extra session different for Mrs F. from that in the case of Mr S. in the previous example?

It had been a feature of Mrs F.'s whole life that she had always been seen as the strong and self-reliant person, upon whom everyone else could lean. She felt she must never let anyone know of her frightened and dependent self. Instead, she usually tried to hide this in order to preserve some contact with others, whom she experienced as leaving her whenever she showed signs of being needy. She had relied on medication to help her in this hiding. When suppression still did not obliterate her feelings, she increased the dose to the point of nearly obliterating herself. Her suicide bid, therefore, was an attempt at finally eliminating those feelings which she could no longer manage alone.

If I had followed Mrs F.'s own diagnosis, that people could not cope with her when she felt most needy, and that she must therefore have stronger medication, I would have been colluding with her phantasy about the unmanageable quality of her own most difficult feelings. Instead, it made more sense to challenge her limiting of herself to only one session a week. At a time when she most expected me to be unwilling to remain in touch with what she was feeling, I offered to be more available to her. She now had a chance, in her therapy, to re-experience the time of her disowned neediness of childhood with me representing her mother who was still expected to retreat from her. This aroused new memories, to do with her search for substitutes for her mother's presence (the dummies), and her finding a security in her mother's sleeping presence – a secret dependence that felt safe because her mother had been unaware of it.

Mrs F. gradually dared to draw upon my availability openly, rather than secretly, and the effect of this 'relationship-holding' was startling. She began to discover that her own most difficult feelings of distress could be contained within a relationship. Of course we had much further work to do, around this hesitant new move towards allowing herself to rely upon someone else again. Nevertheless, it became quite clear that my firmness about her need for more time with a person helped her to feel held by me, rather than seeking relief solely through medication.

Over a period of several months, Mrs F. began to develop a different kind of security, now based upon her use of an outside dependability which she could internalize and consolidate within herself. Her new-found strength was different from her life-long self-sufficiency. Her earlier precocious maturity, arrived at defensively to protect her over-burdened mother, could now give place to a more solid maturity that was arrived at differently. This time it could be achieved at her own pace, rather than at the pace of others; and it was more resilient than brittle.

Some years later, when her husband died suddenly, this progress was dramatically confirmed. The patient's GP once again offered Mrs F. tranquilizers, to alleviate her immediate distress; but she told him quite firmly that she would prefer to arrange a visit to see her therapist. This she did, and allowed herself once again to be analytically held in a relationship in which she felt understood – while she began to mourn this loss she had previously so much dreaded.

Containment by insight and interpretation

A potential admission to mental hospital

Example 6.4

This example concerns the patient who had been sent away from home by her mother when she had refused to eat. (See also Chapter One, example 1.1.)

One day Mrs P. came to a session in a state of uncontrolled alarm. She began talking to me before she had even left the waiting room. She was talking very fast, with increasing loudness until she was actually screaming. The gist of what she was saying was that things were getting out of control at home. She felt unable to cope. She couldn't go on. Her husband didn't understand. 'He just sits there being so bloody calm there doesn't seem to be any way I shall ever get through to him.' She then screamed at me (as loud as she was able): 'IT NEVER GETS ANY BETTER! WHAT CAN I DO? YOU DON'T CARE EITHER.' At this, she picked up a cushion and threw it at me; but she immediately came across to my chair and took it back. She held the cushion close to her and started to cradle and rock it in her arms.

During this episode I was literally sitting on the edge of my chair, wondering what I could do; I felt the patient might need to be hospitalized. However, although she had initially been in a state of uncontrolled desperation and panic, after she began to cradle the cushion in her arms she became calmer.

Internal supervision: I was hearing about the patient not being able to 'get through' to someone. I realized she was probably anxious she might be unable to get through to me too. I therefore reviewed what was happening, in the light of what else I knew about Mrs P., as I knew she had been in a similar agitated state a number of times before.

I recalled that she had been sent to a psychiatric hospital, on a previous occasion. This was after her mother had died: she had then become suddenly overwhelmed by feelings of panic. Her husband had been away. Even when he was called back, her panic had not become any more manageable. The general practitioner had been called in, and he in turn had asked the local mental hospital to provide the containment that seemed impossible at home.

This memory prompted another. As a child, this patient had been sent away from home when she had become very distressed, after her brother was born. She had begun to refuse food, and her mother became unable to cope with this on top of looking after the new baby. She had therefore arranged for Mrs P. (then aged four) to be looked after in a children's home.

When I remembered this I felt on familiar ground. Mrs P. had been creating a specific impact on me, which she almost certainly had on others at crucial times such as those I had remembered during this session. Those others may not have been able to cope with what her distress made them feel. Their response in each case had been to send her away.

Mrs P. had been stirring up in me similar thoughts of sending her away; in fact I was almost sure that she was expecting this. But, after throwing the cushion at me (away from herself), she had quickly retrieved it and was cradling it in her arms (close to herself). As I wondered about that sequence I began to sense an element of hope along with the more immediate despair. Mrs P. was, in effect, giving me a model of what she was needing from me. She was holding the cushion as a baby would be held. Could I find some way of holding the despairing hurt child in her, so that she did not (this time) have to be sent away?

Once I had recognized these elements of communication in her behaviour, I felt an inner conviction which I decided to put into words. She was still rocking but was quieter, so I felt she was ready to let me speak to her.

> *Therapist:* 'I believe you are showing me what you are most needing just now. You need someone to be in touch with the intensity of those feelings which are making you so afraid.' (Pause.) 'I think you are expecting me to send you away, just like other people have done in the past; but I want to continue to help you with what you are feeling – without sending you away.' (Pause.)

> 'You had to find a way of making me feel how frightening these feelings are to you. Your shouting, and throwing the cushion, were ways of making me feel the anxiety and alarm that you can't bear feeling.' (Longer pause.) 'By holding the cushion close to you now, not leaving it thrown away, I believe you are letting me know that this is what you are needing me to be able to do for you.'

> The patient, earlier so terrifyingly out of control, became calmer and comparatively relaxed. I had been dreading the end of this session, in case she experienced this as a similar sending away. Instead, she collected herself together during the remaining ten minutes, thanked me and said she felt better. She would see me at her next session.

Discussion: In order to find a way of containing this patient, it had been essential that I could recognize the unconscious hope expressed in the patient's behaviour. The dynamic operating here was communication through projective identification as I have come to understand it.

If I had not been familiar with this process (which is so often at work in patients who are in search of relationship-holding) it is highly likely that I too would have called in a doctor. But had I done so, under these circumstances, I would have confirmed this patient's phantasy that her distress might always end up being too much for any person to cope with, reinforcing her dread of rejection based on earlier failures to contain. With each similar rejection this phantasy would have become more deeply rooted and difficult to deal with.

The intensity of impact, from patients like this, is often a measure of the frequency with which earlier attempts at finding *containment by a person* have failed. I believe that some mental-hospital patients may be casualties from being too often let down by people who could not contain them, resulting in an assumption that they cannot safely express the intensity of their feelings to any other person. And if someone ever dares such a patient once again to hope, that person can expect to be tested repeatedly for the anticipated failure and rejection.

So, if we are realistically unable to see this kind of patient through the testing times, it is probably better we should not offer to try. It is only when the therapist can survive being tested, to the 'bottom of the trough' and out again, that this new experience can begin to expunge the deep impression of past experience.

With some damaged patients we take on a terrible responsibility. We could make things worse for them if we fail to survive at the point when they most need to test our capacity for survival. So we should only offer containment in a relationship, as an alternative to medication or to hospital containment, with a full awareness of the risks that may be involved. We must know what we could be taking on.

A fear of violence

Example 6.5

This is an example of a patient using his own particular form of communication by impact, whereby he loudly demonstrated his search for containment and the effects on him of his earlier failures to find this.

Mr E. came for a consultation after being turned away by a number of other people to whom he had looked for help. He was in his thirties and therefore younger than me. He was also taller (well over six foot) and obviously stronger. So his presence alone had an impact which was soon to be greatly enhanced by his manner.

In the course of telling me about how he had been referred for therapy, he began to shout and to bang the arm of his chair with a barely contained violence. I could, however, sense that what was being expressed was only a part of this man's violent feelings. The greater part was being held in with a fierce control, which was a major feature of this man's life. His thoughts, he had been telling me, were filled with murderous phantasies. His life was being ruined by his need to keep these feelings under constant check.

What follows was all shouted at me; some of it yelled at me:

> *Patient:* 'You are just sitting there. I know... You are going to do just the same as everyone else. You don't want to help me. You think that I am incurable. They all say that. They listen to me very politely, just like you, and then they show me the door. They think I am violent. I AM NOT A VIOLENT MAN. I have insight into my problems, but nobody believes me. YOU DON'T BELIEVE ME DO YOU? You think I need pills. They all want me to take pills. I am not going to take pills. I AM NOT GOING TO TAKE PILLS. That's what you want, isn't it? You would like to send me away to someone who will just give me pills. I may have violent phantasies, but that is different. I AM NOT A VIOLENT MAN. No-one believes me when I try to tell them that.'

Internal supervision: I could feel myself becoming increasingly anxious. I realized that I was on the receiving end of a powerful projective identification; yet I was not sure what exactly was being put into me. It certainly had to do with violent feelings; but my feelings were not violent – *I felt afraid.*

I knew this patient had made several bids to get treatment without success. He had met with people who reacted to him, as Bion would describe, as if they were 'containers afraid of the contained' (Bion 1967b). These repeated rejections must therefore have added to this man's fear of his own violence. Could I cope with it?

> After this spate of shouting I interrupted Mr E.

> *Therapist:* 'You are thinking and speaking for me, based on what you have experienced with other people. I would like to say for myself what I am thinking. You expect me to send you away; but I am not going to send you away. I am going to offer to take you into therapy.

However, I make one condition. I know you have a lot of violent feelings, which you may need to bring into your therapy. You can bring as much violence here as you need to, as long as it is confined to words. If this becomes physical violence, I cannot promise that I will then be able to continue treating you.'

Patient: 'So you are afraid!' (Pause.)

Therapist: 'Yes, you are able to make me afraid of your violence; but I believe it may be precisely that which you need me to be in touch with – without having to send you away. I think it is your own fear of your violent feelings that you are needing me to help you with.'

Mr E. began to calm down. He understood what I had said. I think he recognized, even then, that it was true. He allowed me to treat him; and, even though he could only come to see me once a week, it was possible to contain him in therapy without medication.

Discussion: Right from the start the cues were all there for me, if I could but see them. Fortunately I was able to recognize the missing link, when Mr E. pointed to my being afraid. *I was afraid of his violence and so was he.* I then knew I had to be prepared to be in touch with this fear, if I was going to be able to help him; and he had to find out whether the person he was with could tolerate this. He had tried with other people who may have missed this communication, or had not wished to work with it, but he had not (quite) given up hope that his fear of his own violence might somewhere begin to be contained by another person and found to be manageable.

Psychotic episodes: an extended clinical sequence

Example 6.6

A patient aged twenty-five (Miss W.) was in once-a-week therapy with me. She had been referred to me because her previous therapist was leaving the country, and therefore would be unable to continue seeing her.

That previous therapy had been conducted under supervision. During it Miss W. had experienced a brief psychotic breakdown. On that occasion, she had been hospitalized for six weeks in a mental hospital where her therapist had been allowed to continue to see her. (I shall refer to this as Hospital A.) Although the hospital consultant had wanted to put her on Stelazine he was persuaded by the supervising consultant psychotherapist to maintain Miss W. on Valium alone.

For the following year of that previous therapy, the supervising consultant had recommended that Miss W. might be better contained if her therapy were less intense. This proved to be the case. Therefore, when she was referred to me, I too saw her only once a week.

I had been seeing Miss W. for the whole of the summer term before taking my first holiday break during her therapy with me. I was away for four weeks. When I returned I discovered that she had been admitted to Hospital B., having gone into psychosis during the last week of my absence. Her psychiatrist in this hospital had started her on Stelazine and would not reconsider this, even though I requested that he might consult with Hospital A. where it had been shown that Miss W. could be contained on Valium alone.

On this occasion Miss W. was in hospital for four months. Even though I visited her there regularly, I was consistently unable to get through to her at any feeling level. She seemed wooden and lifeless. She said that it seemed as if she were 'trying to speak to people through cotton wool'.

Towards the end of these four months, I began to feel that I could renew meaningful contact with this patient. She was beginning to have feelings again. When she was about to be discharged, the consultant psychiatrist advised me that this improvement was due to the Stelazine. He reminded me that I am not a doctor, so I would not be able to appreciate Miss W.'s need for this in the way that he could.

When Miss W. saw me back in my consulting room she confided in me that, for six weeks before leaving Hospital B., she had been throwing away her pills instead of taking them. She had felt so removed from other people, while she was still on Stelazine, it seemed to be the only thing she could do. She told me she had not been able to make any use of my visits to her, while she continued to be 'fuzzed up' with pills.

After I had continued seeing Miss W. once a week for two years, her mother died. At the time, she coped with this largely by not letting herself feel anything about it, and she continued to manage her everyday life without being noticeably disturbed.

Then, several weeks prior to my next summer holiday break, I received through the post an envelope containing a piece of paper on which was drawn a very small triangle and a single initial beside it. The writing was noticeably shaky, and reminded me of the 'Stelazine writing' with which I was familiar from the time when Miss W. had last been in hospital. The post mark was close to Hospital A, and the initial was that of Miss W.'s first name.

Upon telephoning Hospital A., I learned that this patient had been admitted there two days before, in a state of psychosis. I was able to speak to her new consultant, who said she too had started Miss W. on Stelazine, but she readily agreed to have this changed to Valium, and for me to visit.

When I saw Miss W. she clearly knew me, even though she was still in a nightmare world of her own. She talked in bursts of words, not all of which were intelligible or coherent. But from this staccato communication I was able to pick up the following:

> *Patient:* 'Yoga...' (Pause.) 'Falling...everything falling...no stopping.' (Pause.) 'Being held...Yoga teacher holding me...' (Pause.) 'In pieces... They wrote to me...the Yoga class...' (Pause.) 'Six months since...hadn't been since... I'm falling again...I can't stop the falling.'

Putting together what I could from this, I began to realize that she was telling me of a visit to her Yoga class, the first since her mother died. The returning theme of falling also reminded me of Winnicott's definition of 'falling for ever' as one of the 'unthinkable anxieties', and 'going to pieces' as another (Winnicott 1965b:58).

With the help of these cues I sensed what may have happened. By going back to the Yoga class, Miss W. had been suddenly hit by an affective realization of her mother's death. This seemed to have thrown her back into a regressed state, in which she became the child who had nobody to hold her. The Yoga teacher had held her physically. She was needing another kind of holding from me. I therefore began to interpret what I believed she was experiencing.

> *Therapist:* 'When you were last at the Yoga class your mother was still alive. You may have been able to delay taking in the fact of her death, until you returned to this class...' (Pause.) 'On going back, I think you suddenly realized how your world had changed since your last time there: the person who once held you as a child is no longer there for you now.' (Pause). 'Your familiar world, in which there always used to be a mother for you, now feels broken into pieces... This has left you feeling that you are falling, with no-one to stop the falling, and no-one to hold you together.'

> *Patient:* (A quiet pause...) 'The falling has stopped now... You are there to hold me together... You have stopped the falling.'

During the space of half an hour, Miss W. went from hallucinating psychosis to being able to remain in touch with her reality. My hunch, that it could have been the realization of her mother's death, proved to be correct. My being able to interpret what she was feeling helped to provide her with the necessary holding. Through this I was able to get in touch with what she was experiencing, and for her not to be left feeling so alone in this. Her unmanageable experience began to become manageable, and she did not need to return to psychosis to avoid the unbearable pain of becoming suddenly aware of being motherless.

Miss W. was kept in hospital for a further ten days, during which time I saw her once more. She was allowed home to her father, for a week's trial period. She then returned to hospital for discharge, and went back to her full-time job. In all, she had been away from her job for only three weeks.

Two days after going back to work Miss W. came to see me. Her father had just died, having had a heart attack. I immediately felt very concerned about her still being able to cope, with so much happening all at once. I recalled the earlier summer break, when she had collapsed into a prolonged psychotic state. We only had two weeks before I would be going away for another summer holiday. All her known supports were being taken from her at once.

I arranged for Miss W. to see me on her way back to her job, after she had been to her father's funeral. When she came I was relieved to see how much more in touch with her feelings she was, compared with the time after her mother's death. She was appropriately upset, and she was able to tolerate being in touch with her feelings. This was quite new.

Because I had earlier been so anxious about how Miss W. might manage during my summer break, I drew her attention to how much better she was coping with this second experience of a death. I told her I had been worried about her having to be alone during the summer, with so much having just happened to her. I told her I now felt she was going to be all right while I was away. I later added that it was almost as if the past few weeks, during which she had come to realize the fact of her mother's death, had in some way prepared her to deal with the death of her father too.

Miss W. came for her last session before my holiday. I soon realized that she was on the edge of psychosis again. I began to wonder what may have triggered this new episode, but she immediately gave me the cue that I needed. She had been feeling quite steady until she had come into my consulting room. She had even been all right at work and in her flat; but she 'began to feel wobbly' *on the way to see me.* I felt prompted to re-examine the interaction between myself and this patient.

Internal supervision: Using trial identification, I re-called the patient's last session. I listened to myself trying to reassure her. She may have seen me as not remaining in touch with her precarious state (I wasn't as anxious about her as she was). At the same time I was unconsciously communicating to her my denied anxiety about her capacity to cope on her own (else why would I be trying to reassure her?). This helped me to offer an interpretation.

> *Therapist:* 'I believe I was unhelpful to you in your last session. I may have put some of my own anxiety into you about whether you would cope during the summer break. When I was trying to be reassuring about this, I think it probably had the opposite effect on you as if I had been trying to brush aside what you were feeling. I know I can only really help you when I am letting myself remain in touch with what you *are* feeling, rather than suggesting you could be feeling some other way.'

> *Patient:* 'I am glad you have realized that. I felt you were rather going on about how I would cope; and I wasn't at all sure I could. Then you seemed to be far away from me. It made me feel all alone again. Now I don't feel so alone.'

Miss W. returned from the edge of further psychosis. I went on my holiday, and she returned to work and stayed there. She did not find the break in her therapy at this particular point at all easy; and yet she coped with it herself – drawing upon new resources that she had discovered in herself.

Discussion: The state of the analytic holding for this patient, at each critical moment in the sequence, was dependent upon the extent to which I was able to be in touch with her. There were different kinds of obstacle getting in the way. When she was on Stelazine she was contained medically; but she could not be reached emotionally, let alone feel held by insight or by a relationship. The medication had created a barrier to her being in touch with her own feelings, or to my attempts at getting through to her. When she was not on Stelazine, the obstacle that began to get in the way was more to do with my uncertainty about her strengths or my ability to contain her.

While I was behaving in a way that unconsciously communicated my own doubts to the patient, and my distance from what she was feeling, then she naturally felt alone with her anxiety. She only began to cope with this again when I indicated that I had picked up her unconscious prompt to me, communicated so clearly during this last session. Only then could the therapeutic holding be resumed, and not before.

Review of examples

In this chapter I have been giving variations upon a theme. We are taught that 'reassurance never reassures'. It is an easy principle to remember, but not always so easy to apply. I have therefore given examples to illustrate some of the dynamics which are operating when we give in to this impulse to use reassurance.

At such moments it is also difficult to put into practice another maxim of technique, that 'the best containment is a good interpretation'. That means being able to make sense of what a patient is saying and feeling, and able to convey this to the patient. It also implies good timing. If an interpretation is accurate in content but poorly timed, it is a bad interpretation; it can even be experienced by the patient as persecutory.

Analytic holding therefore is always based upon a capacity to tolerate being genuinely in touch with what the other person is feeling, even to the extent of feeling those feelings oneself. There must also be some way of making interpretive use of the feelings induced in the therapist by a patient.

However, any interpretation based upon impact should include an awareness of why the patient has needed the therapist to experience what he has been feeling. If it is not yet possible to see this as purposeful communication, there is a serious risk that the therapist will respond unhelpfully by *avoidance* or by behaving in a way that is experienced by the patient as a *retaliation*. The patient is usually expecting one of these responses, based on past failures in relationship.

Patients have taught me that when I allow myself to feel (even to be invaded by) the patient's own unbearable feelings, and if I can experience this (paradoxically) as both unbearable and yet bearable, so that I am still able to find some way of going on, I can begin to 'defuse' the dread in a patient's most difficult feelings.

In summary, therapists have to be able to interpret as well as contain. Passive containment is not enough, as it feeds a phantasy of the therapist being made unable to continue functioning as therapist. Interpretation alone is not enough, particularly if it can be experienced as the therapist maintaining a protective distance from what the patient is needing to communicate. Psychotherapeutic technique has to be able to bring together these two functions, in such a way that the patient can experience a real feeling-contact with the therapist and yet find that the therapist is able to continue functioning.

A therapist's capacity to provide a patient with this analytic holding is discovered through the real (and recognized) survival of that which the patient experiences as the worst in himself or herself (Winnicott 1971:Chapter 6).

Note

1. I am not confining myself to Bion's view of containment, but it may be useful to have a description of that. In his book *Splitting and Projective Identification*, Grotstein says of this:

> 'Bion's conception is of an elaborated primary process activity which acts like a *prism* to refract the intense hue of the infant's screams into the components of the color spectrum, so to speak, so as to sort them out and relegate them to a hierarchy of importance and of mental action. Thus, containment for Bion is a very active process which involves feeling, thinking, organizing, and acting. Silence would be the least part of it.'
>
> (Grotstein 1981:134)

7

Analytic holding under pressure

I now wish to give a clinical example where containment became an issue of such central importance that the outcome of the analysis depended upon it. As always, it is when an analyst or therapist is under stress that analytic holding comes to be most tested.

When pressure from a patient is extreme there are two pitfalls in particular that need to be avoided. One is for the therapist to look for security in a rigid adherence to the usual rules of technique; but patients do not feel secure with a therapist being defensive in this kind of way. The other is for the therapist to feel justified in stepping outside the analytic framework, in order to accommodate to the special circumstances; and yet patients usually sense a therapist's alarm when extra-ordinary ways of working are resorted to.

Occasionally, however, we may have to introduce an exception. When we do, we should anticipate the implications of this for the patient and follow closely the subsequent repercussions (see Eissler 1953).

In order to illustrate this dilemma, I shall present a further sequence from the analysis of Mrs B., several months after that described in Chapter Five.

Background to the clinical sequence

After Mrs B. had re-experienced the accident (when she had been burned by boiling water), I imagined there could be no worse thing for us to encounter in her analysis. I was thinking of what Winnicott had said: 'There is no end unless the bottom of the trough has been reached, unless *the thing feared has been experienced*' (Winnicott 1970:105).

I did, however, know that Mrs B. had been operated on at the age of seventeen months, under a local anaesthetic, to release growing skin from the dead scar tissue left from her burns. I also knew that the mother had fainted during that operation, leaving her child confronted by the surgeon who continued with the operation regardless. A memory of this experience had suddenly erupted into consciousness, at a time when Mrs B. had been feeling particularly unsupported in her marriage; and she had recalled thinking that the surgeon was going to kill her with his knife. At the time of the operation, she seems to have absented herself from this unmanageable experience by going unconscious. (It had, in fact, been the distress of this memory that had first prompted Mrs B. to look for psychoanalytic help.)

Even though I knew the details of that early memory, I believed it did not compare with the experience of the accident, which had been brought into the earlier session. I wanted to think we had already negotiated 'the bottom of the trough'.

The clinical sequence[1]

Soon after the summer holiday Mrs B. presented the following dream. *She had been trying to feed a despairing child. The child was standing and was about ten months old. It wasn't clear whether the child was a boy or a girl.* Mrs B. wondered about the age of the child. Her son was soon to be ten months old. He was now able to stand. She too would have been standing at ten months. (That would have been before the accident.) 'Why is the child in my dream so despairing?' she asked. Her son was a lively child, and she assumed that she too had been a normal happy child until the accident.

I felt prompted to recall how Mrs B. had clung to an idealized view of her pre-accident childhood. Was she now daring to question this? I therefore commented that maybe she was beginning to wonder about the time before the accident. Perhaps not everything had been quite so happy as she had always needed to assume. She immediately held up her hand, signalling me to stop.

During the following silence I wondered why there was this present anxiety. Was the patient still needing not to look at anything from before the accident unless it was seen as perfect? Was the accident itself being used as a screen memory? I thought this probable. After a while, I said she seemed to be afraid of finding any element of bad experience during the time before the accident, as if she still felt the good that had been there before must be kept entirely separate from the bad that had followed. She listened in silence, making no perceptible response for the rest of the session.

The next day, Mrs B. came to her session with a look of terror on her face. For this session, and the five sessions following, she could not lie on the couch. She explained that when I had gone on talking, after she had signalled me to stop, the couch had 'become' the operating table – with me as the surgeon who had gone on operating regardless after her mother had fainted. She now could not lie down 'because the experience will go on'. Nothing could stop it then, she felt sure.

In one of these sitting-up sessions Mrs B. showed me a photograph of her holiday house, built into the side of a mountain with high retaining walls. She stressed how essential these walls are, to hold the house from falling. She was afraid of falling for ever. She felt this had happened to her after her mother had fainted.

Mrs B. had previously recalled thinking her mother had died, when she had fallen out of her sight during the operation. Now, in this session, she told me one part of that experience which she had never mentioned before.

At the start of the operation Mrs B.'s mother had been holding her hands, and she remembered her terror upon finding her mother's hands slipping away as she fainted and disappeared. She now thought she had been trying to re-find her mother's hands ever since.

Mrs B. began to stress the importance of physical contact for her. She said she was unable to lie down on the couch again unless she knew that she could if necessary hold my hand, in

order to get through this re-living of the operation experience.
Would I allow that or would I refuse? If I refused she wasn't
sure she could continue with her analysis.

My initial response was to acknowledge to her that she
needed me to be 'in touch' with the intensity of her anxiety.
However she insisted she had to know whether or not I would
actually allow her to hold my hand. I felt under increased
pressure, due to this being near the end of a Friday session,
and I was beginning to fear that the patient might indeed leave
the analysis.

My next comment was defensively equivocal. I said that
some analysts would not contemplate allowing this, but I
realized she might need to have the possibility of holding my
hand if it seemed to be the only way for her to get through this
experience. She showed some relief upon my saying this.

Over the weekend, I reviewed the implications of this
possibility of the patient holding my hand. While reflecting
upon my countertransference around this issue, I came to
recognize the following important points: (1) I was in effect
offering to be the 'better mother', who would remain holding
her hand, in contrast to the actual mother who had not been
able to bear what was happening; (2) my offer had been partly
motivated by my fear of losing the patient; (3) if I were to hold
this patient's hand it would almost certainly not, as she
assumed, help her to get through a re-experiencing of the
original trauma. (A central detail of this had been the *absence*
of her mother's hands.) It would instead amount to a bypassing of this key factor of the trauma, and could reinforce
the patient's perception of this as something too terrible ever
to be fully remembered or to be experienced. I therefore
decided that I must review with the patient the implications of
this offer, as soon as I had an opportunity to do so.

On the Sunday, I received a hand-delivered letter in which
the patient said she had had another dream of the despairing
child, but this time there were signs of hope. *The child was
crawling towards a motionless figure, with the excited expectation of
reaching this figure.*

On the Monday, although she was somewhat reassured by
her dream, Mrs B. remained sitting on the couch. She saw the

central figure as me, representing her missing mother. She also stressed she had not wanted me to have to wait to know about the dream. I interpreted her fear that I might not have been able to wait to be reassured, and she agreed. She had been afraid I might have collapsed over the weekend, under the weight of the Friday session, if I had been left until Monday without knowing she was beginning to feel more hopeful.

As this session continued, what emerged was a clear impression that Mrs B. was seeing the possibility of holding my hand as a 'short-cut' to feeling safer. She wanted me to be the motionless figure, controlled by her and not allowed to move, towards whom she could crawl – with the excited expectation that she would eventually be allowed to touch me. Mrs B. then reported an image, which was a waking continuation of the written dream. She saw the dream-child reaching the central figure, but as she touched this it had crumbled and collapsed.

With this cue as my lead I told her I had thought very carefully about this, and I had come to the conclusion that this tentative offer of my hand might have appeared to provide a way of her getting through the experience she was so terrified of; but I now realized it would instead become a side-stepping of that experience *as it had been* rather than a living through it. After a pause I continued. I said I knew that, if I seemed to be inviting an avoidance of this central factor of the original experience, I would be failing her as her analyst. I therefore did not think I should leave the possibility of holding my hand still open to her.

Mrs B. looked stunned. She asked me if I realized what I had just done. I had taken my hand away from her just as her mother had, and she immediately assumed this must be because I too could not bear to remain in touch with what she was going through. Nothing I said could alter her assumption that I was afraid to let her touch me.

The following day, the patient's response to what I had said was devastating. Still sitting on the couch, she told me that her left arm (the one nearest to me) was 'steaming'. I had burned her. She could not accept any interpretation from me. Only a real physical response from me could do anything about it. She wanted to stop her analysis, to get away from what was happening to her in her sessions. She could never trust me again.

I tried to interpret that her trust in her mother, which had in a fragile way been restored after the accident, seemed to have been finally broken after her mother had fainted. It was this ultimate breach of that trust which had got in the way of her subsequent relationship to her. I felt that it was this she was now in the process of re-enacting with me, in order to find that this unresolved breach of trust could be repaired. She listened, and was nodding understanding, but she repeated that it was impossible to repair.

The next day, Mrs B. raged at me still for what she saw as my withdrawing from her. The possibility of holding my hand had been the same to her as actual holding. She felt sure she would not have abused the offer. It had been vitally important to her that I had been prepared to allow this; but my change of mind had become to her a real dropping away of the hand she needed to hold onto. To her, I *was* now her mother who had become afraid. Her arm seemed to be on fire. To her, I was afraid of being burned too.

Mrs B. told me that the previous day, immediately after her session with me, she had become 'fully suicidal'. She had only got out of this by asking a friend if she could go round to see her, at any time, if she felt that she couldn't carry on. She had not ultimately needed to see her friend; it had been her friend's availability which had prevented her from killing herself. She rebuked me with the fact that her friend could get it right. Why couldn't I?

I told her that she did not need from me what she could get from others. She needed something different from me. She needed me not to buy off her anger by offering to be the 'better mother'. It was important I should not be afraid of her anger, or of her despair, in order that I stay with her throughout the re-lived experience of not having her mother's hands to hold onto. (Pause.) She also needed me to remain analyst, rather than have me as a 'pretend' mother. It was therefore crucial I do nothing that could suggest I needed to protect myself from what she was experiencing or was feeling towards me. She listened and became calmer. Then, momentarily before leaving the session, she lay down on the couch. She thus resumed the lying position.

I shall now summarize the next two weeks. Mrs B. dreamed of *being lost and unsafe amongst a strange people with whom she could not find a common language*. I interpreted her anxiety as to whether I could find a common language with her. In one session she had a visual image of a child crying stone tears, which I interpreted as the tears of a petrified child (herself). She dreamed of *a baby being dropped and left to die*. She dreamed of *being very small and being denied the only food she wanted; it was there but a tall person would not let her have it*. In another dream *she was in terror anticipating some kind of explosion*.

Throughout this, she persisted in her conviction that she could never trust me again, and she experienced me as afraid of her. Alongside this, she told me her husband had become very supporting of her continuing her analysis, even though he was getting a lot of 'kick-back' from it. This was quite new. I interpreted that, at some level, she was becoming more aware of me as able to take the kick-back from her in her analysis.

Shortly after this Mrs B. reported the following two dreams in the same session. In the first *she was taking a child every day to meet her mother to get some order into the chaos*, which I interpreted as her bringing her child-self to me, in order to work through the chaos of her feelings towards me as the mother she still could not trust. She agreed with this, but added that she didn't bring the child to me by the hand. She had to drag her child-self by the hair.

In the second dream *she was falling through the air, convinced that she was going to die despite the fact that she was held by a parachute with a helicopter watching over her*.

She could see the contradictions (sure of dying whilst actually being safe) but this did not stop her feeling terrified in the dream, and still terrified of me in the session. She stressed that she did not know if I realized she was still feeling sure she was dying inside.

On the following Monday Mrs B. told me she had dreamed that *she had come for her last session as she could not go on. She had begun falling for ever, the couch and the room falling with her. There was no bottom and no end to it.*

The next day the patient felt that she was going insane. She had dreamed *there was a sheet of glass between herself and me, so that she could not touch me or see me clearly. It was like a car windscreen with no wipers in a storm.* I interpreted her inability to feel that I could get in touch with what she was feeling, because of the barrier between her and me – created by the storm of her feelings inside her. This prevented her seeing me clearly, just as it had with her mother. She agreed and collapsed into uncontrolled crying, twisting on the couch, tortured with pain. At the end of this session, she became panicked that I would not be able to tolerate having experienced this degree of her distress.

On the Friday, she spoke of a new worker in her office. She had asked him how long he had been trained. She then realized she was asking him for his credentials. I interpreted her anxiety about my credentials, and whether I had the necessary experience to be able to see her through. I added that maybe she used the word 'credentials' because of the allusion to 'believe'. She replied: 'Of course, credo.' She said that she wanted to believe I could see her through, and to trust me, but she still could not.

The next week, Mrs B. continued to say she did not think she could go on. She had had many terrible dreams over the weekend. The following day she again sat up for the session. Intermittently, she seemed to be quite deluded – with her awareness of reality fleeting and tenuous.

For the greater part of the session she was a child. She began by saying she doesn't just talk to her baby, she picks him up and holds him. Then, looking straight at me she said: 'I am a baby and you are the person I need to be my mother. I need you to realize this, because unless you are prepared to hold me I cannot go on. You have got to understand this.' She was putting me under immense pressure. Finally, she stared accusingly at me and said: 'You *are* my mother and you are *not* holding me.'

Throughout this I was aware of the delusional quality of her perception of me. (I now understand this in terms of the psychic immediacy of the transference experience.) There was little 'as if' sense left in her experience of me in this session, and at times there seemed to be none. It was meaningless to her when I attempted to interpret this as transference, as a re-living of her childhood experience. Not only was I the mother who was not holding her; in her terror of me I had also become the surgeon with a knife in his hand, who seemed to be about to kill her. At this point there appeared to be no remaining contact with me as analyst.

Internal supervision: I reflected upon my dilemma. If I did *not* give in to her demands I might permanently lose the patient from the analysis, or she might really go psychotic and need to be hospitalized. If I *did* give in to her I would be colluding with her delusional perception of me, and the avoided elements of the trauma could become encapsulated as too terrible ever to confront. I felt placed in an impossible position. However, once I came to recognize the projective identification process operating here, I began to surface from this feeling of complete helplessness. This enabled me eventually to inter-pret from the feelings engendered in me by the patient.

Very slowly, and with pauses to check that the patient was following me, I said to her: 'You are making me experience in myself the sense of despair, and the impossibility of going on, that you are feeling... I am aware of being in what feels to me like a total paradox... In one sense I am feeling that it is impossible to reach you just now; and yet, in another sense, I feel that my telling you this may be the only way I can reach you.'

She followed what I was saying very carefully, and slightly nodded her head. I therefore continued: 'Similarly, I feel as if it could be impossible to go on; and yet, I feel that the only way I can help you through this is by my being prepared to tolerate what you are making me feel, and still going on.'

After a long silence Mrs B. began to speak to me again as analyst. She said: 'For the first time I can believe you, that you *are* in touch with what I have been feeling; and what is so amazing is that you can bear it.'

I was then able to interpret to her, that her desperate wish for me to let her touch me had been her way of letting me know that she needed me to be really *in touch* with what she was going through. This time she could agree. She remained in silence for the last ten minutes of this session, and I sensed it was important I should do nothing to interrupt this.

The next day, Mrs B. told me what had been happening during that silence. She had been able to smell her mother's presence, and she had felt her mother's hands again holding hers. She felt it was her *mother from before the fainting* she had got in touch with, as she had never felt held like that since then.

I commented that she had been able to find the internal mother she had lost touch with, as distinct from the 'pretend' mother she had been wanting me to become. We could now see that if I had agreed to hold her physically it would have been a way of shutting off what she was experiencing, not only for her but also for me, as if I really could not bear to remain with her through this. She immediately recognized the implications of what I was saying, and replied: 'Yes. You would have become a collapsed analyst. I could not realize it at the time, but I can now see that you would then have become the same as my mother who fainted. I am so glad you did not let that happen.'

To conclude, I will summarize part of the last session of this week. Mrs B. had woken feeling happy and had later found herself singing extracts from the Opera *'Der Freischütz'*, the plot of which (she explained) includes the triumph of light over darkness. She had also dreamed *she was in a car which had got out of control having taken on a life of its own. The car crashed into a barrier which had prevented her from running into the on-coming traffic. The barrier had saved her because it had remained firm. If it had collapsed she would have been killed.* She showed great relief that I had withstood her angry demands. My remaining firm had been able to stop the process which had taken on a life of its own, during which she had felt completely out of control.

The same dream ended with the patient *reaching out to safety through the car windscreen, which had opened to her like two glass doors.*

Discussion

This case illustrates the interplay between various dynamics. My initial offer of possible physical contact was, paradoxically, tantamount to the countertransference withdrawal which the patient later attributed to me in my decision not to leave the offer of the easier option open to her. In terms of Bion's concept of 'a projective-identification-rejecting-object' (Bion 1967b:Chapter 9) the countertransference here became the container's fear of the contained.

The resulting sequence can be understood in the inter-actional terms of Sandler's concept of role-responsiveness (Sandler 1976); or in terms of Winnicott's description of the patient's need to be able to experience in the present, in relation to a real situation between patient and analyst, the extremes of feeling which belonged to an early traumatic experience but which had been 'frozen' because they had been too intense for the primitive ego to encompass *at that time* (Winnicott 1958:281).

There had come to be a real issue between this patient and me, in the withdrawal of my earlier offer of the possibility of holding my hand. In using this to represent the central element of the original trauma, the patient entered into an intensely real experience of the past as she had perceived it. In so doing she was able, as it were, to 'join up with' her own feelings, now unfrozen and available to her. The repressed past became, in the present, a conscious psychic reality from which (this time) she did not have to be defensively absent. During this, I had to continue to be the surviving analyst, and not become a collapsed analyst, in order that she could 'defuse' the earlier phantasy that it had been the intensity of her need for her mother that had caused her mother to faint.

The eventual interpretive resolution within this session grew out of my awareness of the projective identification process then operating. I sensed that the pressures upon me related to the patient's desperation being unconsciously aimed at evoking in me the unbearable feeling-state which she could not on her own yet contain within herself

It is a matter for speculation whether I would have been so fully subjected to the necessary impact of this patient's experience had I not first approached the question of possible physical contact as an open issue. Had I gone by the book, following the classical rule of no physical contact under any circumstance, I would certainly have been taking the safer course for me; but I would probably have been accurately perceived by the patient as afraid even to consider such contact. I am not sure that the re-living of this early trauma would have been as real to the patient, or in the end so therapeutically effective, if I had persisted throughout at that safer distance of classical 'correctness'.

Instead, I acted upon my intuition; and it is uncanny how this allowed the patient to re-enact with me the details of this further trauma, which she needed to be able to experience within the analytic relationship and to be genuinely angry about. It is this unconscious responsiveness, to unconscious cues from the patient, to which Sandler refers in his paper 'Countertransference and Role-Responsiveness' (Sandler 1976).

With regard to the recovered analytic holding I wish to add one further point. Because this was arrived at experientially with the patient, rather than by rule of thumb, it did more than prove a rightness of the classical position concerning no physical contact. *En route* this had acquired a specificity for the patient, which in my opinion allowed a fuller re-living of this early trauma than might otherwise have been possible.

I conclude with two quotations from Bion's paper 'A Theory of Thinking'. There he says (my italics):

> 'If the infant *feels* it is dying it can arouse fears that it is dying in the mother. A well-balanced mother can accept these and respond therapeutically: that is to say in a manner that makes the infant feel it is receiving its frightened personality back again but in a form that it can tolerate – the fears are manageable by the infant personality. If the mother cannot tolerate these projections the infant is reduced to continued projective identification carried out with increasing force and frequency.'
>
> (Bion 1967b:114-15)

> 'Normal development follows if the relationship between infant and breast permits the infant to project a feeling, say, that it is dying into the mother and to reintroject it after its sojourn in the breast has made it tolerable to the infant psyche. If the projection is not accepted by the mother the infant feels that its feeling that it is dying is stripped of such meaning as it has. It therefore re-

introjects, not a fear of dying made tolerable, but a nameless dread.'

(Bion 1967b:116)

Bion is here describing an infant's relationship to the breast. A similar process, at a later developmental stage, is illustrated in the clinical sequence I have described. I consider that it was my readiness to preserve the restored psychoanalytical holding, in the face of considerable pressures upon me to relinquish it, which eventually enabled my patient to receive her own frightened personality back again, in a form that she could tolerate. Had I resorted to the physical holding that she demanded the central trauma would have remained frozen, and could have been regarded as perhaps for ever unmanageable. The patient would then have reintrojected not a fear of dying made tolerable, but instead a nameless dread.

Note

1. This chapter is a revised version of my paper 'Some Pressures on the Analyst for Physical Contact during the Re-Living of an Early Trauma', which was presented at the 32nd International Psychoanalytical Congress, Helsinki, July 1981, and first published in the *International Review of Psycho-Analysis* 9:279-86.

8

Processes of search and discovery in the therapeutic experience

Since Strachey, it has been widely accepted that the only 'mutative interpretation' is a transference interpretation. Strachey says:

> 'It follows from this that the purely informative "diction-ary" type of interpretation will be non-mutative, however useful it may be as a prelude to mutative interpretations. Every mutative interpretation must be emotionally "imme-diate"; the patient must experience something actual.'
>
> (Strachey 1934:150)

While I accept this as true, I believe there are other important dynamics also involved in the process of analytic recovery. In this chapter, therefore, I wish to explore in particular the patient's *unconscious search* for the therapeutic experience that is most needed; and how trial identification and internal supervision help the therapist to distinguish what is healthy in this search from what is pathological.

The therapeutic experience

It is my thesis, here, that the nature of a patient's experience of the therapeutic relationship is at least as important a thera-peutic factor as any gain in cognitive insight. It is within this relationship that there can be new opportunities for dealing with old conflicts, for recovering what had been lost, for finding what had been missing in earlier relationships.

A patient also has a chance to use the therapist in ways that may not have been possible in other relationships. When, for instance, earlier bad experience is transferred onto a social relationship, the recipient of that transference will usually not understand what is happening. So, instead of being able to offer understanding or containment, the other person is more likely to respond to the transference attitudes being taken personally.

Alexander (1954) recognized that patients frequently use the analytic experience in order to deal with unresolved conflicts under new circumstances. He therefore pointed out that, if the analyst's reactions to a patient are too similar to those of the parents, this can lead to a mutual involvement in the patient's transference neurosis, which (in extreme cases) could develop into a *folie à deux*. He also noted that, when the transference neurosis has developed, the analyst feels himself to be placed in a role of the patient's choosing. He suggested the analyst should consciously choose to respond in ways that are opposite to the manner in which the parents had behaved, arriving at this role by a 'principle of contrast'. But this deliberate adopting of a role, in relation to the patient, becomes a way of influencing what he or she experiences in the analysis. In that sense it infringes the patient's autonomy and is antithetical to the analytic process.

Winnicott understood this difference very well. He spoke instead of the patient *finding the object* and *using the object* (Winnicott 1971:Chapter 6). He recognized that there is in every patient an unconscious awareness of the experiences which need to be found, to be re-lived in the transference. Patients therefore look for opportunities in an analysis, to get in touch with previously unmanageable experiences. In the transference, therefore, the analyst is frequently used to represent an earlier relationship, about which there continue to be unresolved feelings. The analyst's mistakes likewise may be used to represent earlier bad experience (see Chapter Five).

The nature of the patient's search

When patients seek out psychotherapeutic help it is often because parents, or other caretakers, have previously failed to respond adequately to various signals of distress. There is often a continuing unconscious hope of finding somebody able to respond to the patient's indications of search. These cues are similar to those of childhood, some of which may have been unacknowledged or left unheeded.

I believe that clinical experience and infant observation both support a notion that there could be (from birth) an innate search for what is needed for survival, for growth and healthy development.[1] It is when this search is frustrated or interfered with that we encounter 'pathological' response; and yet, even in this response there is a healthy pointer to needs which have not been adequately met.

I am here making a distinction between *needs that need to be met* and *wants*. At birth there is no distinction. With the development of a capacity to tolerate increasingly manageable degrees of frustration, growth-needs begin to be differentiated from wants. A small baby 'wants' the mother because the mother's presence is needed. As well as expressing libidinal needs to be fed, to suck or to bite etc., there will be growth-needs. Initially these will be very basic, such as the need to be held, to be related to and played with, and to be enjoyed.[2] In meeting these elemental needs the mother is preparing the foundation for her infant's subsequent growth and development.

In due course, an infant's growth-needs begin to include the need to discover manageable degrees of separateness. And later, there comes a time when the growth-need is for confrontation and a firmness that does not lose touch with caring. This will often be tested by tantrums, which aim to re-instate the infant's earlier control over the mother, because a child does not wish to recognize any distinction between needing and wanting. Hence, the intensity of wanting in a tantrum may seem very desperate. But, when the timing is appropriate to a child's growth, there is also a search for a parent who cares enough to be able to tolerate being treated as bad for saying 'No' when it could be so much easier to say 'Yes' (Casement 1969). Through finding the necessary firmness a child also finds security. When this is not found, a child's demands may be gratified but it is always a hollow triumph. The child is left feeling insecure, and *more* needy not *less*.

Patients re-enact these different stages of growth in the course of therapy. The therapist should therefore try to distinguish between libidinal demands, which need to be frustrated, and growth-needs which need to be met. I believe that some therapeutic opportunities are missed when therapists fail to recognize when it is growth-needs which are being presented for necessary attention. For instance, some patients need to have evidence of having had a real impact upon the therapist; or a patient may need confirmation of valid perception of the clinical reality that this perception is not just phantasy or transference. A patient is let down if a therapist dutifully frustrates these needs, thinking that this is automatically required as a matter of analytic technique.

Even though the patient may look for what he or she needs the therapist is usually regarded as the expert, the one who should know best. In one sense he has to accept this responsibility. It is therefore quite usual for the management of therapy to be thought of as being entirely in the therapist's hands, and that it should in no sense be left to the patient. After all (it could be argued) where might it lead if patients were to be allowed their head in how their therapy should be conducted? Might this not result in the therapist falling into a collusion with the patient? Might it not play into a patient's pathology, offering inappropriate gratification rather than insight? And, was it not partly to avoid such pitfalls as these that Freud insisted that an analysis should be conducted in a state of 'abstinence' (Freud 1914:165)? He was well aware of repressed libidinal strivings in every patient. It was these that he insisted should not be gratified in analytic treatment, for in gratifying them the work of analysis is by passed.[3]

In some patients I have encountered a remarkable sense of what it is that they are unconsciously looking for in therapy; but the manner of a patient's search is often not direct or easily identified. Sometimes there are obvious clues to what is needed. At other times, growing despair of finding this may be indicated by a pressure for further substitute gratification, as if this may be all that could be hoped for. Nevertheless, in this pressure it is often possible to recognize what has been missing for the patient.

When there has been a lack of adequate structure, within which a patient could have more securely negotiated key developmental phases of growth, there is a *search for structure* in the therapeutic relationship. When there has been a lack of sufficient responsiveness in the person taking care of an infant, without which the infant's attempts at communicating pre-verbally were experienced as hopeless or without meaning, there is a *search for responsiveness* in the therapist. When there has been a lack of mental or emotional privacy, within which a child can begin to establish a viable separateness from the mother (or other adults), there is a *search for space.*

For example, patients who have needed privacy and confidentiality will often indicate from the start their fear that this will not be found even in therapy. Or, a patient who has experienced relationships in which there have been inadequate personal boundaries will demonstrate the need for a firmer sense of boundaries in the therapy. This may be communicated directly in the patient's anxiety about not finding this, or indirectly through behaviour that would become uncontainable without an adequate firmness from the therapist. Also, when patients' autonomous thinking has been interfered with by others being too ready to think for them, they will often be passively compliant to the therapist's interpretive activity. Conversely, they may demonstrate an anxiety about being 'seen into', or their thoughts not being private to themselves – even in a silence. In ways like these, patients often demonstrate what they are needing to deal with in the course of therapy, by bringing the effects of earlier pathogenic experience into the therapeutic relationship.

A mistaken use of corrective emotional experience

Some therapists imagine they can provide a patient with better experience, and that this in itself will be therapeutic. This is reminiscent of Alexander's notion of 'the corrective emotional experience' (Alexander 1954). But, in doing so, they fail to allow an analytic freedom to use the therapist in those ways that relate to the earlier experience and inner world of the patient. For instance, when a patient has unresolved feelings about failures in parenting, it becomes intrusive (deflective and seductive) if the therapist *actively* offers himself or herself as the 'better' parent.

Example 8.1

A female patient came into analysis having had some therapy before with a female therapist. The problem she presented, in asking for analysis, was that in her work she was unable to cope with people not liking her. She was a social worker, and it was in particular with her clients that she had this difficulty. She would unconsciously deflect anger, or manoeuvre people back into liking her, and this was getting in the way of her being able to work more effectively.

When this patient had previously entered therapy she had been suicidally depressed. She ended that therapy feeling she had been greatly helped by her warm and encouraging therapist. She had been personally acknowledged and valued. She had also changed her job upon the therapist's recommendation, being persuaded that she would be good at working with people.

Comment: It should be said that this is not analytic psychotherapy. And yet, some people who do work analytically also seem to think that this 'benign' leading of the patient might sometimes be appropriate.

The former therapist had met the patient's need for recognition and for being valued, which had been significantly missing in her childhood relationships. However, it had later begun to dawn on the patient that she had never been able to be angry with her therapist. She then realized that, whenever she had begun to get angry with her therapist, she seemed to take this personally, or she would interpret the anger as relating to someone else.

The patient had always had problems with her anger, and with people being angry with her. Now she found herself taking personally any sign of anger from her clients. As a result, she would try to 'woo' them into feeling better about themselves or about her. She knew no other way.

What emerged in the course of this patient's analysis was that she needed to find an analyst who did not prevent her treating him in terms of her earlier relationships, and especially those about which she felt most angry. It was important that her transference use of the analyst should not be deflected, because she needed to be able to get as angry with him as she felt – in order to discover whether he could tolerate being on the receiving end of those feelings she had learned to regard as damaging.

Her parents had been the kind of people who could not cope with anger. It had left her feeling her own anger to be in some way bad and dangerous; and her former therapist had left her with that impression unaltered. The underlying problems, to do with her self-image as apparently bad or destructive, had not been attended to.

Discussion: The former therapist had made the patient feel temporarily better, by actively reassuring and encouraging her to feel she was a worthwhile person. This illustrates what has sometimes been called a 'countertransference cure'. It may have been the therapist's personal feelings for this patient that had made her feel better, in which case this would have been brought about by means of a charismatic influence and not by any analytic process. In so far as the patient had got better *for her therapist* the benefit had not been long-lasting.

In my opinion, if the other therapist had used internal supervision to question the basis of the patient's improvement, it might have highlighted the extent to which this had been achieved through compliance and a 'false-self' suppression of the patient's more difficult feelings. It is always necessary to be aware of the possibility of this kind of false recovery.

What is also significant in this example is that the therapist's countertransference (which may have included a need to be liked) seemed to parallel the patient's own difficulty in relationships. This might have been why the patient felt she had not been helped with this particular problem in that earlier therapy.

The therapist's non-intrusive availability

Patients, given the chance, will find their own form of relating to the therapist. In this sense, we could compare a therapist's availability to the patient with the use of a spatula in Winnicott's child consultations. He regularly demonstrated that, if an infant is allowed a 'period of hesitation' to notice and to find an unfamiliar (and potentially interesting) object left within view of the infant and within reach, this object will come to be invested with interest-value. It will eventually be spontaneously reached for. The object that he used happened to be a shiny surgical spatula (Winnicott 1958: Chapter 4).

When an infant is not hurried to find this object, it comes to be invested with such interest or meaning as fits in with the infant's readiness to explore this or to play with it. The spatula may be sucked, bitten, 'fed' to the mother, used for banging, for throwing away, for being retrieved by the mother, etc. How this object will be used by an individual infant could not be predicted. Only one thing is certain, that an infant's use of the spatula will never be confined to the use for which it was designed.

If, on the other hand, a child *is* hurried, then this object does not acquire meaning invested in it by the infant. Instead, it remains (or becomes) an alien object belonging to the world of adults, rather than being an object that could be discovered and taken into the infant's world of phantasy and play. Any attempt, therefore, to insert the spatula into an infant's mouth would result in a protest against accepting this intrusive object. The strength of this protest can be regarded as a measure of the healthiness of the child. A less healthy response would be for the spatula to be accepted with passive compliance, or only a token resistance.

If therapists are to avoid being experienced by the patient as an 'impinging object', as with the spatula, it is important that they should be ready to wait for relating and understanding to emerge in the patient's own time. This includes waiting for the transference to develop, through the patient's investment of this unknown person with such meaning as belongs to the patient's internal world. The therapist is there to be 'found' by the patient. If, however, the therapist's way of being with the patient is over-active or intrusive, then interpretation and the therapist's presence can each become an impingement for the patient.

The evolution of the therapeutic process will only be a creation of the patient, which it needs to be, if the therapy is set up from the beginning with minimum influence or pre-conception from the therapist. To that end the therapist tries to keep himself (as a person) as little in evidence as can be in keeping with this aim of preserving the therapeutic space, as neutral and therefore free to be used in whatever way belongs to the therapeutic needs of the patient.

A patient's use of the therapist's availability

Example 8.2

A female patient came for her first session after a holiday break. She arrived ten minutes late, and explained to her therapist (a man) that there had been a lot of traffic on the way which had held her up. She poured out details of what had happened to her since her last session. She had been feeling unsupported by her husband, having had to cope with the demands of the children on her own and they had been very difficult.

Internal supervision: The therapist sensed that the patient was alerting him to the possible impact upon her of the holiday break. Because of the pressure to talk, which was the most obvious aspect of her communication, he continued to listen.

The patient gave further examples of feeling alone, having no-one to turn to, feeling cold, etc. There were still no pauses in her narrative.

The internal supervision: The therapist was beginning to feel redundant in the session, in that the patient was not leaving any room for comment, and he wondered whether he should intervene to make his presence felt. But, lacking any clearer cue from the patient, he chose to remain silent.

After further out-pouring of holiday details the patient began to describe an incident with her husband. He had been depressed recently and unresponsive. She was feeling in particular need of his support one night, but he didn't reach out to her – even when she was crying. After a pause she added: 'He didn't even speak to me.'

There was a slight pause in the flow of talk from the patient at this point. The therapist, therefore, took his cue from her silence and used the themes presented to provide a bridge towards eventual interpretation.

> *Therapist:* 'You have been telling me details of what you have been dealing with since your last session. You now tell me about somebody who has been depressed, who did not respond to you; and you add that he didn't even speak to you.'

Comment: The therapist is replying to the patient from a position of unfocused listening. He therefore does not focus the patient's anxiety immediately upon himself; that would be pre-emptive. Instead, he leaves room for the patient to make her own reference to him, if she is ready for this. The potential link to the therapist is left, like the spatula, within reach of the patient for her to use this in her own way or to ignore it. This guards against a transference interpretation being thrust at her.

> *Patient:* 'I was beginning to wonder why you weren't saying anything. It occurred to me that perhaps you were sorry to be back at work, or you might be feeling depressed.'

> *Therapist:* 'I realized you were anxious, but I was waiting to see if you could let me know more about this.' (Pause.) 'I think you may have been trying to let me know about your own depression, which you have been needing somebody to be in touch with; and the holiday break has added to your sense of being left to deal with this alone.'

The patient began to cry: the flood of her talking had stopped. After a while she began telling the therapist about her mother's moods, when she was small. There had been times when the patient could not find any way to get through to her mother, who had been too preoccupied with her own depression.

> *Therapist:* 'I think you may have experienced my absence during the holiday, and my silence in this session, as reminders of being with your mother – her distance from you and your difficulty in being able to get through to her.'

The patient recalled more about her relationship to her mother, and began to get angry with the therapist for being like her. By the end of the session, however, the patient was able to notice that her therapist was not being defensive or retaliatory in response to this anger. Her closing comment was: 'I expected you to object to my being so angry with you.'

Discussion: Here we have an example of a therapist who is prepared to wait, to be found by the patient in whatever way that happens. The patient is therefore not prevented from making use of him to represent a bad experience in childhood. Having attacked him for being like her mother she finds that he has remained unchanged by this. So, through this non-retaliatory survival of her treating him as a 'bad object' she re-discovers the therapist as a 'good object'.

It is all too easy to cut across a patient's spontaneous finding of the therapist's presence by intervening too quickly. A similar error is to bring the patient's communications to a premature focus onto the therapist, which is often done in the name of transference. This deadens the experience by lessening the sense of immediacy in the transference. By not allowing more time for this to develop in the session, a patient can be blocked from arriving at the more specific details that are often contained in a patient's further associations (if these are not interrupted).

It also deflects from the patient's *experience of feelings* towards *thinking about feelings*, before the actual experience has been more fully entered into. This invites the patient to intellectualize and can also be evidence of a countertransference defensiveness on the part of the therapist. When this happens, patients will often respond to this as a cue from the therapist to avoid what may have been difficult for the therapist to stay in touch with for longer.

Patients' differing needs

When therapists discover their patients' capacity for sharing in the therapeutic process, they have much to gain from learning to recognize the different levels of prompt. This does not mean that a therapist merely follows where patients lead, nor does it mean that patients are simply given what they ask for (or demand). It also does not mean that all such demands should be systematically frustrated, as if these were always pathological. Neither therapist nor patient alone can know what is best or what is needed. This is jointly discovered as the therapeutic process unfolds.

Therapists, therefore, must learn to distinguish between a patient's healthy strivings in the therapeutic process and pathological resistance to this. And they have to be able to recognize when a patient's perception is valid, even when this is critical of the therapist. It might not just be a further manifestation of projection or transference.

A discipline which I find useful, in listening to what a patient communicates, is to scan for what I might *least* want to hear as well as hearing what I may be anticipating. This helps to counter-balance the residual effects of pre-conception. It also helps to highlight precisely those issues which countertransference anxiety may prompt me not to recognize.

Mistakes and corrective cues

When something happens in a session that does not fit in with a patient's unconscious sense of what he or she needs to find in the therapy, there are various ways in which this may be indicated. This can be thought of as a 'countertransference interpretation' by the patient (Little 1951:39), as the patient's 'potential therapeutic initiative' (Searles 1975:97), as the patient's 'unconscious supervision' of the therapist (Langs 1978), or as unconscious prompts. It can become a central issue to an analysis or therapy, to what extent a therapist is able to be responsive to these unconscious cues from the patient.

Inevitably, any analyst or therapist is going to make mistakes. It is therefore important to be able to recognize when this is happening; and it is a function of internal supervision to help in precisely this. When a therapist regularly uses trial identification to review his own part in a session, or in the therapy as a whole, he will discover how often patients give unconscious cues that indicate when something is wrong in the therapy. However, what is more important than a mistake having been made is coming to realize this and doing something about it. How a therapist deals with the effects of his own mistake(s) can become an important part of the therapeutic process itself. If a therapist fails to recognize when he is making mistakes, the patient comes to be cut off from his or her part in this process.

It is, therefore, a tragic loss when patients offer corrective cues to a therapist, but find these thrown back unrecognized for what they are. Some therapists are too ready to interpret all communications from a patient in terms of assumed pathology (in the patient) or as resistance to insight (as given by themselves). The patient's unconscious endeavour to help the therapist can then be defensively ignored.

Forms of prompting

Some patients are quite clear when things do not feel right in the therapy, and they are able to point this out consciously and directly. Other patients communicate their criticism of the therapy less consciously.

There are several ways in which unconscious criticism is communicated. Perhaps the most familiar is through a patient's use of *displacement*. Some other person such as a parent, a figure of authority or a person who should know better, may be criticized. Often this can be recognized as alluding to a recent issue in the therapy.

Another form of unconscious prompt is when a patient uses what could be regarded as *criticism by contrast*. It may be that another professional is described as having done a careful job, in the context of the therapist having been unwittingly careless. The patient may be unconsciously holding up a model of better functioning, which it behoves the therapist to recognize as a possible cue to some area of his own poor functioning. Therapist and patient alike can benefit from adaptive responses by the therapist to this kind of corrective cue from the patient.

One other form of unconscious prompt, that is more difficult to recognize (or easier to overlook), is when a patient uses *introjective reference* as a more concealed form of unconscious criticism. By introjectively identifying with an aspect of the therapist, the patient blames himself for something which can be more meaningfully understood as referring to the therapist.

The patient described in Chapter Three demonstrated each of these forms of unconscious prompting, in the course of the sequence described.

The absence of pressures upon the patient

Even though it is generally accepted that the analytic space should be preserved as far as possible from any kind of personal influence, or other pressures, there remains an element of unacknowledged pressure in the application of the 'basic rule' which is often applied in analytic psychotherapy. Therapists are usually taught to explain to patients *there is only one rule, that of free association:* that a patient is to say whatever comes to mind, regardless of what it is. When the patient fails to comply with this rule it is frequently interpreted as 'resistance'. It can easily be overlooked that this resistance is sometimes a response to the basic rule.

It is interesting that traces of Freud's earlier 'pressure technique' remain in his use of the 'rule' of free association. Although this was regarded as the only rule, it nevertheless contains an implied pressure – in saying to patients that they should learn to use free association, and at the same time suggesting that this 'free' association should itself be subject to a pressure to speak and to say all. Some patients become stuck on exactly this issue, particularly those patients who have been denied a sense of separateness and privacy in childhood. It can therefore be a growth-promoting experience for a patient to find a mental and emotional space (within a relationship) that is genuinely free from external pressures. A patient's inability to be free in this way can sometimes be a prompt for the therapist to re-consider the application of this 'basic rule', and the notion of resistance in relation to this.[4]

There are many other forms of pressure that can be introduced by the therapist, and patients frequently give unconscious cues that relate to this. I shall give some examples below (see examples 8.5, 8.6 and 8.7).

Establishing the therapeutic boundaries

Example 8.3

When a patient (aged twenty-two) came for her initial consultation she immediately poured out an account of her life till then. Throughout this, there was a repeating theme to do with people who did not respect the personal boundaries of others. Her parents had been intrusively controlling of her life; her uncle had made sexual advances to her as a child; her doctor was a family friend, and had a reputation of flirting with his patients. While saying this, the patient became anxious and reached for a cigarette. She found that she did not have any matches and asked me whether I could give her a light.

I felt alerted by what the patient had already told me. I therefore said that I realized she was anxious, and might want to use a cigarette as a way of dispelling some of her difficult feelings, but there were other issues at stake. For instance, she had been telling me about people who had failed to keep to the boundaries necessary to each of the relationships she had been describing. Most recently there had been this doctor-friend who flirted with his patients. So, I felt she may be unconsciously checking out something about me, whether I could maintain a professional relationship without this being blurred by gestures that could be confused with a more social kind of relationship.

Once this patient had started therapy it became clear how important to her it had been that I made this stand right at the beginning. She often referred back to this as basic to her eventual trust in me. This was all the more crucial to her at times when she was needing to use me to represent those others who had mis-used her.

Maintaining the boundaries

Example 8.4

A patient (Mr H.) had started therapy some months before a summer holiday. He had not mentioned having his own holiday already arranged; but when the time approached for my holiday he told me he would be leaving a week earlier than me. This presented me with a dilemma. When I am making the initial arrangements for therapy I also give my holiday dates: if these clash with arrangements already made by the patient, this is usually discussed at the time. We had not discussed this overlap of dates.

I knew that Mr H. had felt deserted by his previous therapist, who had become ill during a holiday break and had not resumed therapy with the patient. He might, therefore, need to have a clearer sense of continuity over the first break in this therapy – particularly as it was going to be extended by his prior absence. I decided to explore the patient's feelings about this, and to clarify the fee arrangement for his missed week of therapy.

> *Therapist:* 'I would not normally charge you for sessions missed because of arrangements made prior to starting therapy; but I realize you may have feelings about your sessions being kept for you while you are away. I am therefore wondering what you would like us to do about the three sessions you will miss.'

> *Patient:* 'I would like to have those sessions before I go away.'

Internal supervision: I was reminded that when Mr H. first came to see me he had been wondering about having four sessions per week, but had started with three. Was he perhaps wanting to come more frequently, prior to going on holiday, as a way of helping him to decide whether to shift his therapy to four sessions a week on a more permanent basis? I prepared to explore this possibility.

> *Therapist:* 'I am not yet sure I will be able to make that arrangement, but we could look into the possibilities and the implications.'

Mr H. thanked me. After a short pause he told me about a previous job he had been at, where it had been necessary to take holidays by a certain fixed date in the year or you would miss your holiday. He added the comment: 'It was inconvenient in some ways, but at least you knew where you were.'

He went on to emphasize his need for regularity in his life, and illustrated this by saying his ulcer usually comes back when that stability has been lacking. He is careful what he eats and has to eat regularly.

Internal supervision: I felt I was being cued to recognize the implications for Mr H., if I were to offer him those extra sessions as suggested.

> *Therapist:* 'I think you are pointing out to me that, even if I were able to see you for the extra sessions before you go away, it could be a mixed blessing. You seemed grateful at my offer, but you have since been pointing out to me that you become anxious, even unwell, when there is a lack of stability in your life. A shift in the arrangements concerning your therapy could have exactly that sort of effect upon you.'

Mr H. was thoughtful, and then agreed he needed to know where he was with me. This was more important, in the long run, than having extra sessions.

A therapist becomes intrusive with a premature interpretation relating to himself

Example 8.5

A female patient, who was seeing a male therapist, had missed several sessions without explanation or getting in touch.

Upon returning, the patient said she had really not missed the sessions at all; she had been too busy with other things. She hadn't missed her ex-boyfriend either; she felt better off without him. He just wasn't important to her any more.

> *Therapist:* 'I think you may be wondering how important I am at this moment in your life too.'

> *Patient:* 'No, you are very important. I couldn't do without you at the moment. I have had more important things to do recently, so I have had to give therapy a lower priority. That's all.' (Pause.)

> 'I got very angry with someone I hardly know recently. This guy came back to our flat after a party. I was irritated with the way he kept butting in on our conversation. It wasn't as if he had really been invited; he had just tagged on when we left the party, and when he did not get the attention he was wanting he had the nerve to change the TV channel without even asking. I then just blew my top.'

Discussion: The therapist arrives at his comment without a firm link between what the patient had been saying and any possible reference to the therapy. He presumes to know what the patient is thinking, so his interpretation becomes an intrusive intervention.

If we trial-identify with the therapist here, he might be feeling badly treated, perhaps even wondering how important he was to the patient. What he says comes across as if he had arrived at this interpretation from his countertransference feelings, and it sounds like a projection of his own doubts. Similarly, if we trial-identify with the patient, we can recognize that the analytic space is being intruded upon by the therapist, who appears not to want to be ignored by the patient.

The patient's response is two-fold. She first reassures the therapist that he need not doubt his importance in the patient's life. She then speaks of an incident where someone (else) had been intrusive. We may be hearing an unconscious commentary (Langs 1978) from the patient, upon the nature of the therapist's intervention as perceived by the patient, and an account of irritation and anger felt towards him.

Although the sequence described by the patient had occurred before this session, the timing in the session (i.e. when she thinks of it) is telling. The therapist was able to recognize himself being rebuked here by the patient, and could acknowledge his awareness of this later in the session. This is a good example of unconscious supervision by the patient. See also below.

A therapist becomes inappropriately directive

Example 8.6

The patient, a girl aged twenty-five, was being treated by a female therapist.

> *Patient:* 'I cannot stand the pressures at work. I think I may have to find another job.'
>
> *Therapist:* 'Have you ever thought of going to a careers advice centre?'
>
> *Patient:* 'I was thinking about that myself, but I don't think I should need to be given advice about what to do with my life. I ought to be able to get in touch with that within myself.' (Pause.) 'I only came back to London after the summer holiday because of you, but I now feel angry with you for some reason.' (Pause.) 'My boss will be back tomorrow. I know what it will be like: he will be constantly telling me what to do – interfering pressure all the time. He never seems to see me as able to do things for myself.'

Discussion: We can see here an example that is filled with corrective cues from the patient. She did not need the therapist to be thinking for her. She also feels that she does not need to be given advice, as she ought to be able to get in touch with her own sense of direction from within herself. That is what the patient has been used to getting in her therapy, and here she feels the therapist is out of role. The patient then appears to change the subject, and we hear about somebody (referred to as her boss) who will be telling the patient what to do. The patient is assumed to be unable to do things for herself.

If we apply unfocused listening to this it is not difficult to pick up the displaced criticism. She is angry with her therapist, for becoming too like other people in her past (and present). She needs to be allowed to use the analytic space more freely than that.

Difficulties in getting through to the therapist

Example 8.7

A female patient aged thirty was seeing a male therapist.

> *Patient:* 'I am having difficulties in communicating. I feel lonely even when I am with other people. I feel at a distance from David (her husband). I was angry with him today, but we then made love. That was just before I set out to come here. I didn't actually want sex; I have difficulty in saying 'No' or in showing how I am really feeling. It helped to push my angry feelings down, but they don't go away.' (Pause.) 'I miss my old boss. I only had to raise my eyebrows and she would realize when I needed to speak to her.' (Pause.) 'Why do you think I have these difficulties?'
>
> *Therapist:* 'It probably goes back to your childhood.'
>
> *Patient:* 'Which relationship? Do you mean my parents?' (Lots of childhood details then followed.)

Discussion: The themes here include various references to difficulties in relating. The patient feels distant and lonely, even when she is in company. (In the session she is with the therapist.) There is anger, and there is an example of anger being by-passed (having sex). There seems to have been a need to get rid of this anger (or sexual feelings?) before coming to her session. There may also be an example of criticism by contrast when the patient refers to another person (her previous boss), who would respond even to a raised eyebrow – picking up indications of need in the patient. The session ends with another example of a flight to the past being introduced by the therapist.

In this session, the therapist could have played back the main themes, in some not yet specific way, in preparation for dealing with the anxieties indicated. He could have said something like:

> 'You have been telling me about feeling not understood and feeling at a distance from the person you are with. You also tell me about feelings that you tried to get rid of before coming here today. I think there may be some anxiety about whether I am able to understand you, and what feels safe for you to bring to your therapy.'

The reason for remaining non-specific, in this play-back of themes, is that we do not know more precisely what this patient is anxious about bringing to her therapy. It may be her feelings of criticism for her therapist. It may be her sense of not being understood. It may be her anger, or her sexual feelings. She allows her husband to deflect her anger: she may be anxious to find out whether her therapist is also someone who feels a need to deflect difficult feelings, or whether he can cope with these being more clearly directed at him.

The therapist's first comment in this session is in response to a direct question. He may have given the patient the impression that he needs more than a raised eyebrow for him to respond. When he then deflects the patient to her childhood, this is likely to confirm her anxiety about the effect of her difficult feelings upon other people. So, when the patient compliantly examines her childhood relationships, at the safe distance of time-past, she may well be reflecting her perception of the therapist. He could be seen as defending himself from the difficult allusions to him in the opening part of this session.

(A few weeks after the sequence given here this patient left her therapy.)

In this chapter I have tried to illustrate some of the many ways in which patients contribute towards the shaping of their therapy, and towards helping the therapist to provide the kind of therapeutic experience which they are needing to be able to discover. And when things are going wrong, patients offer many unconscious cues to the therapist to draw attention to this – for the analytic hold to be re-established and the analytic process resumed.

Therapists need to recognize the element of healthy searching within a patient's unconscious. If they can adequately distinguish between growth-needs and pathological striving, then they may discover the gradual process whereby a patient unwittingly guides the therapist towards what is unconsciously looked for within the therapeutic relationship. It is in this kind of way, when something is amiss in the therapy, that patients will often nudge the therapist back towards ways of working that are nearer to what is needed by that patient, at that moment in that therapy.

Notes

1. In speaking of an innate search for what is needed, I realize that this issue is more complex than I imply in the main text. I do not wish to overlook that an infant's perception of the 'object' is distorted by his or her own feelings, by the aggressive or 'death' instinct, by the splitting of good and bad, by the projection of bad feelings into the 'feeding object', and by a multiplicity of other complicating factors. These get in the way of any easy finding of what is needed, or easy providing of it.

2. Winnicott speaks of 'ego-needs' which are very similar to the growth-needs as described here (Winnicott 1965b:Chapter 4).

3. Since writing this, the paper by Fox 'The Concept of Abstinence Re-Considered' (1984) has been published. The author advocates a more discriminating application of the technical concept of abstinence. Part of his argument is based upon a discussion of the clinical sequence given above in Chapter Seven, as previously published (Casement 1982).

4. Analysts have been slow to drop the practice of giving the 'basic rule' to patients, even though it has been realized that this can create resistance. Over thirty years ago, Margaret Little said: 'We no longer "require" our patients to tell us everything that is in their minds. On the contrary, we give them permission to do so' (Little 1951:39). In many training institutions the 'basic rule' still seems to be given.

9

The search for space: an issue of boundaries

I now wish to illustrate more extensively the part played by a patient's unconscious cues, and how these contributed to the effectiveness of the resulting analysis.

I had to discover how to read the cues of this patient, which I did by trial-identifying with her or with the objects of her relating. From this way of listening it was possible to recognize what the patient was needing that she had not been finding. She dramatically demonstrated her need for clear boundaries to the analytic relationship, and for a genuinely neutral space in which she could become autonomously herself.

Introduction

Miss K. (as I shall call the patient) was aged twenty-seven when she was referred to me. She had suffered for years with compulsive eating.

For the greater part of her short analysis (twenty months) Miss K. subjected me to severe testing, acting out with others what I would not enter into with her. Outside the analysis she continued to be engaged in attempts at getting alternative help, all of them alien to the analysis. I had to maintain a difficult balance between trying to contain this acting out (which I could only do if I were to interpret this as attacks upon the analysis) and having to be careful not to get caught into repeating the responses of those who had previously been trying to control this patient's life.

Miss K. gave me many unconscious cues for handling her analysis. These were given in the account of her past life, and in the details of her acting out. It was very clear to me what had not helped her, and what was still not helping her. By contrast, I could sense what she was most deeply searching for. I therefore tolerated the acting out (not that I had much option) and I continued to seek an understanding of it through interpretation. This meant, however, that I had often to tolerate being put into a position of apparent analytic impotence, with the analysis seeming to be quite chaotic.

What emerged, after many months of this near annihilation of the analysis, was that it was in my non-retaliatory survival of this testing by the patient that the potency of the analysis ultimately lay. She came to discover that the analysis continued to offer her an un-biased relationship-space in which she could begin to become her 'own version of herself'. (This phrase occurred in one particular interpretation and was adopted by the patient as a central theme of her analysis.) She did not have to offer a compliance to please. Neither did she have to maintain, indefinitely, her protest against the pressures that had always been upon her to comply.

Having found this neutral space in the analysis, Miss K. began to use it in preparation for how she would be later. For the first time in her life, she was able to own herself and find an independent life apart from the family's expectations of her. The duration of this analysis had to be time-limited due to visa restrictions on the patient's length of stay in this country. Nevertheless the progress made has been maintained since, already over a number of years.

Practical limitations on the analysis

Because of the uncertainty about her length of stay in this country, I felt that I could not offer Miss K. five-times-a-week analysis immediately even though she was asking for this. I therefore waited until it was known how long she could remain here.

I originally saw Miss K. in twice-weekly therapy. This was increased to four times per week once it became clear that she earnestly wished to have analysis as the treatment of choice rather than just 'having more'. I had to be careful that it did not become another form of compulsive eating, having everything that was available in order to gratify her insatiable hunger. I eventually agreed that analysis, even short-term, could give her the optimum chance of finding the help she needed.

I saw Miss K. for four sessions a week during most of her first year of treatment with me. When her visa position was clarified she knew she could stay for a maximum of a further eight months. For the remaining time I saw her five times per week.

It was during this latter period that Miss K. began to use her analysis in a quite different way; whereas, throughout the first year, there had always been a possibility she might have to leave the country at short notice. She had therefore been constantly fighting against letting herself experience yet another relationship with any degree of dependence, knowing how difficult she had always found separation in the past. She was afraid there could again be an abrupt ending, without time to work through her feelings about it.

The family background

In the early part of her analysis the patient poured out details of unhappy relationships and experiences. She came from a moderately well-off Jewish family, which she described as dominated by the mother who was said to be manipulative and intrusive. The patient has a sister two years younger than herself.

Miss K. spoke of her relationship with her father as one of close mutual attachment. She recalled being alarmed when her mother began threatening to leave him, because she was going to take the children with her. She experienced her mother as 'stifling', choosing her friends and preventing her from having any real independence. Her father, a business-man, had died suddenly from a heart attack when Miss K. was seventeen. This event was followed by the patient's first period of over-eating.

Miss K. had been breast-fed until after she had cut her first teeth. My impression was that her mother may have wished to prolong the breast-feeding, and it could have been the biting that prevented this. Later, it seemed as if the mother felt that *she* had been deprived by the separateness achieved through this weaning, and it may have accounted for some of the pressures upon Miss K. to behave in her habitually placatory (and compensatory) way towards her mother – trying to make her feel all right. It would also throw some light upon the importance of biting in the patient's subsequent attempts to establish a fuller separation from her mother.

There had been a natural predisposition toward an oral fixation, probably encouraged by her mother's flamboyant enjoyment of breast-feeding. She had openly boasted that this had been more satisfying to her than any part of her marriage relationship.

When Miss K. was just two years old she had to give up her mother to a baby sister. There was some suggestion that her mother may have been depressed after the sister's birth. At any rate, the mother withdrew from the home 'for a rest after the birth', leaving both children with a nanny.

Miss K. became gripped by jealousy towards her younger sister and regularly turned to her father for comfort. He seems to have received her over-intimately. For instance, when she was distressed he would get into her bed to comfort her, and I was told he continued this up until he died. Miss K. felt bereft and empty after her father's death. It was then that she first turned to regular over-eating, in an attempt to deal with her grief and depression.

This quasi-sexual attachment to her father (tinged as it was with a sense of 'Oedipal triumph' over her mother) had in no way been resolved before he died. Instead, that experience became a prototype for her relationships to men. She therefore regarded her sexuality as uncontainable, as if this had been responsible for destroying the much needed structure of her parents' marriage. Equally, she saw her sexuality as overwhelming to any object of her love, even life-threatening, and therefore to be avoided. She expected men to retreat from her. The first important boyfriend who did not immediately retreat also had a heart condition.

To add to this confusion about her sexuality, her mother had also behaved seductively towards her daughters. I was told that when Miss K. and her sister had reached puberty her mother would make them lie in bed with her, and she would stroke their developed breasts. She had taunted Miss K. by laughing at her and saying 'You're a lesbian'.

Her mother's own sexual orientation sounded confused and confusing. She had started an affair with another man before the father had died, but this affair, like the marriage, had been unstable. When her mother was upset by this she would turn to Miss K. for solace. There had also been a strange 'aunt', during the patient's early adolescence, with whom her mother would go on holiday without the children. Miss K. wondered whether this woman was a lesbian, and it left her wondering whether her mother had been bisexual.

Miss K. described her difficulties in forming relationships with boyfriends, discovering herself to be manipulative and possessive like her mother. Whenever she was attracted to a man, she became overwhelmed by her feelings and would crave to be loved. She also found that her boyfriends became impotent with her, blaming this on her. At least one boyfriend had described her as 'devouring'. She had again turned to food in an attempt to deflect this relationship-hunger, which she regarded as being too much for any person to satisfy. For most of her analysis, it was precisely this anxiety that I was having to cope with in her relationship to me.

Issues relating to over-eating

Because the eating problem was so over-determined, it will simplify my account of this if I consider it in relation to various aspects of the patient's life.

The mother's ambition for her daughter was for her to be 'slim and beautiful' and to get married. Outwardly, Miss K. accepted these goals as her own, but there was a much stronger wish to thwart her mother's ambitions. She felt that if she allowed herself to remain thin, which she had been during her early puberty, it would be tantamount to her ceasing to be a separate person. Her mother seemed to 'own' her, as if trying to live vicariously through her.

Miss K. discovered that over-eating was one way of demonstrating a separateness over which her mother could have no control. This provoked active concern (even wailing) in her mother, that gratified Miss K.'s ambivalent wish to be demonstrably separate from her and yet still the centre of her mother's interest. However, she did not see the dynamics of this rebellion against the mother until she was in analysis.

In her mother's company Miss K. usually found she was unable to be angry. Instead, she became desperate to please, and fearful that her mother might prefer her younger sister to herself. Even when Miss K. was in England, away from her mother, she would frequently write placatory letters or telephone her – often daily. At the same time she felt her mother to be like a 'cancerous growth' inside, of which she felt she could never rid herself.

The mother was skilled in putting on an act of being hurt: 'How could you do this to me after all I have done for you?' etc., and she became very upset if Miss K. ever hinted that her mother might not be the most loving mother possible. Miss K., therefore, could only express her angry feelings by turning these against herself and the internalized mother. When she over-ate she quite specifically chose to eat 'rubbish food', experiencing a sadistic pleasure in 'throwing all that garbage at my mother inside'.

Because of the highly sexualized relationship with her father, who seemed to have given her little sense of appropriate parent/child boundaries, Miss K. had come to experience any physical contact with a man as incestuous. Her mental image of any boyfriend easily merged with that of her father. She therefore felt guilty about heterosexual physical contact, and one function of her eating was to make herself 'physically repulsive' (her own phrase). By thus discouraging the sexual contact, which consciously she craved for, she managed to avoid this incest guilt.

Miss K. also wondered if she could more successfully avoid feeling guilty in a homosexual relationship, but even there she felt trapped by the incestuous implications of her mother's sensual seductiveness towards her. The way felt blocked for her in either direction. She could not allow herself to be genitally sexual without feeling guilty, so she would set up forms of self-punishment – with the unconscious hope that she could thereby allay her guilt about having any sexual feelings at all. For a long time, eating had offered her some kind of compromise and compensation for this lack of genital satisfaction.

The patient had only once or twice experienced orgasm in intercourse, partly due to her infrequent experience of intercourse, and partly because her boyfriends so quickly became impotent with her. She assumed this was because they could not face her insatiable demands. In fact she expected everyone, including me, to retreat from the intensity of her demands upon them.

I never got a clear picture of the patient's sexual life. She did not spontaneously offer to speak of this, and I deliberately chose not to question her.

By putting on a lot of weight, Miss K. could simulate the appearance of being pregnant, and she would phantasize to herself that she was. The significance of this first emerged consciously during the middle part of her analysis, at which time her sister came with her doctor husband to live and work in England. The sister was already four or five months pregnant. Miss K. was invited to live with them. She did, and there were frequent outbursts of jealousy and envy towards the sister and her pregnancy.

Her sister's marriage was already the object of much envy, her sister having 'got a husband' whereas the patient regarded herself as too fat and unlikeable ever to marry. The pregnancy added a further dimension to the tension, with roots which we were able to trace back to the time of her mother's pregnancy with this sister. Miss K. remembered her mother telling her how she, as a small child, had tried to attack her mother's pregnant belly. She had been violently jealous of her sister as soon as she was born. For a long time after the birth she had refused to eat food prepared by her mother, and at times she could only be fed by her father or by someone else not her mother.

During the course of her sister's pregnancy, Miss K. put on weight in parallel with the growth in the pregnancy. To a large extent she succeeded in making herself look as pregnant as her sister, but inwardly she seethed with envy towards her sister's live baby which mocked the sterile fullness of her own belly.

The patient demonstrates her need for boundaries

Miss K. originally came to England, from her home in west-coast America, in pursuit of her former therapist (Dr Z.). She had been in twice-weekly private psychotherapy, with this doctor in America, for nearly two years. That therapy was abruptly terminated when Dr Z. accepted an opportunity to work in Europe. There had been no time to work through that interruption of her therapy.

Miss K. continued to be in touch with Dr Z. during the intervening two years, by letter and by telephone. Her journey to England was a last bid to persuade him to let her resume therapy with him. She telephoned him from London begging him to allow this. She was wanting to find accommodation and work in the town he had moved to. Only then did she accept that Dr Z. was not going to let her resume treatment with him. Instead, he recommended she try group therapy. Miss K. told me that he had explained this recommendation saying: 'the transference to a single therapist would be unmanageably strong.' She felt hurt and rejected by this, but she was not deterred from her search for further individual therapy. She was ultimately referred to me.

During the opening phase of her analysis I heard a lot about Dr Z. At the time of her previous therapy he had been a psychiatric registrar. From the patient's account of that therapy, I gathered that he conditioned her with praise and encouragement. She felt erotically attached to him, and was gratified and excited by his interest in her body. She found that she could manipulate this interest in her, through focusing upon her body-weight. Dr Z. would weigh her every time she went for a session, and he praised her for each loss in weight. He offered further encouragement by describing the kind of clothes which would set off her figure to best advantage, even to the detail of the best kind of bra. Miss K. described one occasion when Dr Z. got her to strip to the waist, to show him how her bust was coming along as a result of the loss of weight (helped by the recommended bra).

The overt relationship focus during that previous therapy was around Miss K.'s boyfriend of the time. She described her therapist as 'masterminding' her relationship with this boyfriend, and she was able to satisfy by these means her wish to be allowed to be 'absolutely dependent' on Dr Z. He even let her telephone him to ask what she should do next in relation to her boyfriend, and Dr Z. would tell her.

Towards the end of her treatment with Dr Z., Miss K. rewarded him by losing a lot of weight; and with his frequent advice and guidance she set about trying to get her boyfriend to propose. It was around this time that Dr Z. told her he was leaving America to work in Europe.

The impending loss of her relationship to this therapist exposed the extent of her erotized attachment to him, and he continued to gratify her demands beyond the time when the treatment relationship 'officially ended'. Apparently, in order to ameliorate her desolation upon losing him, Dr Z. allowed Miss K. to visit him in his family home. She saw him there several times, during the month remaining before he left for Europe, and she told me she stayed overnight on more than one occasion. Being in the spare room next to the main bedroom, she claimed to have listened to Dr Z. having intercourse with his wife.

Comment: A number of points need to be made clear about the patient's account of this previous therapy and of her other activities outside the consulting room.

What she was describing was her perception of those experiences. In her relationship with Dr Z., for instance, we have to bear in mind how her wish to be erotically involved with him would colour her perception of that experience, and how she remembered it. So, should we regard this only as an account of the patient's internal world, and as evidence of an unresolved erotized transference with the distortions of wish-fulfilment? We can certainly see transference elements; but it cannot all be dismissed as transference if the therapist had in reality been gratifying the patient's seductiveness with seductive behaviour of his own. We therefore should not describe the interaction between this patient and her former therapist as *'just* transference' (Leites 1977).

Also, the patient's own basic truthfulness, which was a feature of her analysis, should be taken into consideration. Although she did hide some things from me at first, in her acting out of those feelings which she initially split off and kept separate from the analysis, I found she was always in the end prepared to face the details of her own truth – however painful it might be. Miss K. gave me the impression that she never consciously ducked the truth about herself or distorted this by exaggeration.

Miss K. felt utterly shattered when Dr Z. refused to take her back into therapy. She had been counting on resuming her relationship with him, particularly as she had lost weight 'entirely for him'. She reverted to massive over-eating, and had put on some forty pounds in the last few months before being referred to me. This gain in weight, at that time, was largely motivated by her wish to revenge herself upon Dr Z.

Miss K. continued to be obsessed with her unfinished relationship to Dr Z.; she felt herself to be in love with him. Compared with this, her unhappy relationship with the boyfriend in America (which had since broken down) paled into insignificance. In her revengeful eating she had reached the point where she felt no longer able to control her eating at all. She frequently felt desperate, and close to breakdown. She sometimes felt suicidal, but did not think that she had the courage to be actively suicidal.

Issues related to boundaries

Miss K.'s way of using Dr Z.'s first name made it sound as if she were speaking of a boyfriend rather than a therapist, and this was actually how she felt about him. Dr Z. was kept on a pedestal, and the patient would say: 'At least he showed he cared', whereas I was seen as coldly distant and uncaring.

The psychiatrist who referred Miss K. to me had told her that she needed clear analytic boundaries, if she were to have any chance of making better use of further therapy. Being desperate for help, she gave me (from the start) an outward compliance with the conditions of treatment. She never telephoned me and she never asked for extra time. However, towards other people she continued to express the manipulative and demanding side of herself.

I interpreted this as her way of trying to spare me the intensity of her feelings; and when I was able to see how she was pressurizing others I could see what it was that she was protecting me from. It was also her way of being the good and obedient child, in her relationship to me, with the assumption that she would be rejected if she brought to me those other aspects of herself she was expressing elsewhere.

However, I soon discovered that Miss K. had a strong tendency to provoke others into offering her alternative forms of treatment, in parallel to her seeing me. I therefore had to make an early decision on how to handle this.

I felt the patient was trying to provoke me to adopt a non-psychoanalytic role, so that I might try stopping this acting out against the analysis. By trial-identifying with the patient, to consider this option, I recognized that if I responded in any way aimed at controlling her, she might experience me as repeating a traumatic factor of her relationship with her mother. This convinced me that I would not be able to interpret her experience of me as transference, if she could realistically see me as actually behaving like her mother. I sensed that Miss K. was unconsciously provoking me to re-enact with her the role of an intrusive mother.

Whilst I had to be alert to this splitting of the transference, and ready to interpret it as such, I realized how quickly this patient used all interpretations as if they were attempts by me to manipulate her, to direct her, or in some way to run her life for her. For a long time, she would react to interpretations as if these were disguised directions.

It gradually became clear that Miss K. had virtually no experience of any relationship between two people in which one person was not actively trying to manipulate the other. This soon became a central aspect of her analytic experience. I had to help her to find a personal space in which to discover her own thoughts and feelings, and eventually her own sense of direction, rather than play into her addictive dependence upon others to provide direction for her.

For a time Miss K. found it exceedingly difficult to believe she had any capacity for inner-directedness, and she fought against my frustration of her demands to have her life controlled for her. For instance, she frequently went outside the analytic relationship to get others to give her the advice I refrained from giving. By successfully manipulating others into a directive role towards her, she could bypass the firmness of my stand upon this.

Most particularly, Miss K. was using her brother-in-law (a doctor) as an alternative therapist. He regularly advised her, and arranged other forms of treatment – all of which were expressions of his opposition to psychoanalysis. Her acceptance of these other treatments also expressed her disowned attacks on the analysis.

The first attempts at alternative treatment were through medication. Initially this was prescribed by the GP; but, after her brother-in-law came to England, Miss K. began to accept medication from him. This included anti-depressants as well as appetite suppressants. I was not told about her use of medication until some time afterwards.

The next major attempt by the brother-in-law was to have the patient's jaws wired. This was regarded as an ultimate prevention against her compulsive eating. Miss K. was to have her teeth locked together, so that no food could be chewed, and she would only be able to take in liquid foods. She first told me about this when she had already been to a dentist to have impressions made, in preparation for having this dental procedure.

As with Miss K.'s earlier attempts to provoke me into trying to prevent her acting out against the analysis, I was here put into yet another dilemma. If I tried to interpret this as a further attack upon the analysis, which it so clearly was, it was certain she would hear this as a poorly concealed manoeuvre by me to stop her having her jaws wired. If I had tried then to interpret her assumption that I was trying to control her (as if this were only based upon her other relationship experiences i.e. as transference) this would have carried little conviction.

As I really did want to stop her, I had to be even more careful to let Miss K. make her own decision, whether or not to proceed with the plans already made, without indicating my preference either way.

Miss K. came to her next session with her teeth already wired together. As with her earlier use of medication I was faced with another *fait accompli*. I privately wondered whether she could use this 'contraption' in her mouth (which is how she spoke of it) as something transitional between an external relationship controlling her and the beginnings of an internalized capacity for self-control. When I explored this with her it turned out that she could not.

The dentist's device came to be experienced by Miss K. as an embodiment of her intrusive mother. She felt this object (once fixed in her mouth) to be persecuting her, in trying to force a control upon her, as her mother had. It also became something to be defeated by any means possible.

Miss K. experienced the same kind of hate towards this object as she had often felt for her mother. It intensified her wish to defeat her mother's designs for her, and the designs of anybody else who seemed to be aligned with her mother through their attempts at controlling her.

Even though the wiring of her jaws made it impossible for her to bite anything, she became ingenious in finding ways of bypassing this restriction. She crushed up fattening foods, and would suck the resulting mixture through a wide tube. She continued to put on weight; and I used to hear a note of triumph in her complaints of depression at the failure of this last-resort method of her eating being controlled for her.

Nevertheless, a new discovery emerged, that biting played a key part in her pleasure of eating. Deprived of the direct satisfaction of biting into food, Miss K. became much more openly violent in her biting sarcasm, and her angry snapping attacks upon people who angered her. Much of this was directed towards the brother-in-law, who had advised her to have her teeth wired. Some of it was also aimed at me, as I had not stopped her taking his advice.

During the four months that her teeth remained wired together, Miss K.'s sister gave birth to a daughter. This aroused intense jealousy, and envy of the closeness between the mother and baby. Miss K. only felt able to alleviate this by taking over the baby from her sister, whenever possible. She would thereby come between the baby and the real mother, pretending the baby to be her own. We could see here a remembering, through re-experiencing, of the early phantasies which she had around the time when her mother had given birth to her sister. This also confirmed our earlier interpretive work, concerning the patient's childhood feelings of exclusion from her parent's relationship and from her mother's relationship to her sister.

This acting out of the past in the present was further exemplified when Miss K.'s mother visited England to see her first grandchild. Miss K. became jealous of any attention given by her mother to her sister, or to the baby. She frequently resorted to eating as an attempt to suppress these feelings, but indirectly also to express them.

At about this time the brother-in-law, who had come to regard himself as principally in charge of Miss K's treatment, referred her to a behaviour therapist. This other therapist insisted she should immediately have her teeth unwired, and Miss K. offered herself into his hands for yet another version of being told what to do.

Miss K. was able to act out, in her relationship with this behaviour therapist (whom I shall call Mr R.), her wish for physical closeness from which she unconsciously assumed I needed to be protected. She was able to repeat with him many aspects of her earlier relationship with Dr Z.

Mr R., like Dr Z., took an increasingly physical interest in the weight problem and in Miss K's body as a whole. He also changed from seeing her in his day-time office to seeing her in the sitting room of his home. The rationale behind the treatment that he was offering was to condition Miss K. against certain forms of eating. He also said he wanted her to feel better about her body generally. I shall give two examples.

(1) Mr R. got the patient to lie on the floor (in his home) while he put his fingers in her mouth. He was quoted as saying: 'Now imagine that my fingers are a Mars Bar.' He then encouraged Miss K. to develop phantasies around having a

Mars Bar in her mouth, with the excited anticipation of eating this. After this he inserted his fingers further down her throat to make her 'gag'. The intention here was to create a conditioned-reflex link between eating Mars Bars and an impulse to vomit. What Miss K. did not tell him, however, was that she found the insertion of his fingers into her mouth sexually arousing. She did not want him to stop doing it.

(2) On one occasion Mr R. told the patient she needed to get more used to being touched physically. He apparently proceeded to stroke her body, while she lay on the floor, concentrating mainly upon her breasts. This episode was also in his home. His wife was somewhere around but not in the room. He said that his wife 'fully understood' the necessity for his patients to have this kind of treatment.

The patient told me she found the whole episode both exciting and frightening. She was subsequently in a state of acute conflict over returning to see Mr R. for further treatment. She did not really want him to help her with her eating problems. If she went back, she knew it would be for the sexual arousal involved in it for her. She phantasized about him as a continuation of her relationship with Dr Z. Eventually however, after much hesitation, she made her own decision to stop seeing this latest alternative therapist.

I interpreted mainly in terms of the patient enacting with other people those aspects of her wished-for relationship with me, which she kept isolated from the consulting room. By getting her brother-in-law to act like the intrusive mother, and the dentist with his 'contraption' as an actualization of that, she could keep me as the idealized and therefore non-intrusive mother. Equally, by setting up a quasi-sexual encounter with the behaviour therapist, Miss K. was able to keep me as the safe and non-sexual father.

It was not easy to help Miss K. recognize the multiple ways in which she contributed towards setting up these situations. She would complain about people who would keep telling her what to do, how they would manipulate her life and intrude upon it. However, it was clear to me that in some way she was addictively attached to this kind of relationship. In the analysis too she put pressure on me to offer her active advice and direction, as if this might be the only way for her to cope with the problems of her life. She would go through the motions of complaining about pressures from other people, and trying to fight these off, but she would still use her evident helplessness as a way of eliciting futile attempts at helping her. She could then make these attempts fail, and she would tell me of each failure with unmistakable enjoyment – again with a note of triumph in her voice.

Establishing boundaries

When her mother was in this country, Miss K. at first fell back into the kind of relationship which she and the mother had always been used to. This involved an oscillation between the patient's compliant wish to please and outbursts of anger. These would be followed by regrets and self-recrimination, wishing to patch up the appearance of a good relationship with the mother.

In the course of this visit, however, the patient discovered the extent to which this pattern of relating was based upon a phantasy that her mother needed to be protected from Miss K.'s murderous feelings towards her. She was seeing her mother as not able to let her become fully separate. It gradually became clear that this was her way of trying to hide from herself her own fear of being rejected by her mother. Both mother and daughter were obsessively trying to deny any bad feelings towards the other. As a result one could become separate from the other.

However, during her mother's stay here, Miss K. dared to challenge this relationship and the shared phantasy that separation could not be tolerated. She spoke her mind to her mother in ways she had never previously imagined possible. To her surprise the mother survived this, and did not revert to a manipulative use of hurt feelings. There was, for the first time, a lot of straight speaking by the patient to her mother. This helped to establish a sense of psychological distance between them. She could then point out to her mother some of the occasions when she was still being intrusive; when, for instance, she was expecting to know everything the patient was doing and thinking or feeling.

Miss K. also became more aware of the ways in which she had habitually invited others to become intrusive. She began to see that she did not have to remain the helpless victim of other people's intrusion. Being more in touch with the ways in which she evoked intrusion, she discovered she could modify her own part in this with correspondingly different responses from those around her.

By the time her mother left England, after a visit of about six weeks, Miss K. had started to establish herself as a separate person. Her mother had responded to this and had begun to see this daughter differently. The relationship between them, which before had been so symbiotic and confused, began to become differentiated. In particular, personal boundaries were established between mother and daughter where before there had been none.

We then moved into the final stage of Miss K.'s treatment with me. Once she learned exactly when her visa was due to expire she was able to finalize her plans to emigrate to another country. We had four months' notice of her departure. This precipitated the patient into a new earnestness, wishing to get from her analysis what she needed before she had to leave.

During these remaining months, Miss K. began to realize that her eating had lost a great deal of its earlier compulsive quality. She felt she would eat normally once she had left England, but she deliberately continued to maintain her over-weight while she was still here. She did not want her family, particularly her mother and brother-in-law, to think that any visible progress was in any way due to their pressures upon her if she allowed herself to lose weight while she was still living within their orbit and influence. She regarded this awareness, that her over-eating was beginning to become a redundant habit, as a secret which she shared only with me.

Miss K. decided to leave her analysis the week before she left England. This was a deliberate choice, her wanting to have the experience of knowing she could have had more sessions (during the remaining week) but knowing she had chosen for herself not to. In this way she was able to give to her leaving an important element of her own choosing. It was not just passively accepted, as a time set for her by the authorities around the expiry of her visa; nor was it simply the patient pre-empting the end, though it was that too.

Miss K. used her last session sitting in a chair face to face with me. During this last hour she reviewed what she had gained from her analysis. The statement which stood out most particularly was: 'I am becoming my own version of myself.' She also spoke about the importance of discovering the space between people. She had experienced this for herself and she was confident that she would never forget it.

Discussion of the role of the analyst

The decision to offer analysis

When I began seeing Miss K., and was hearing the account of her earlier therapy, I had urgently to find ways of understanding the responses which she evoked in me. For instance, it was impossible not to feel the impact of her demanding neediness, and I knew that I too might experience this as overwhelming – particularly if I could not find some way of understanding it. Eventually, however, I became convinced that there were important cues here for the management of this patient's analysis.

In reviewing what Miss K. had told me of herself, I could see she had never felt securely contained by her previous therapist, who had probably been subjected to the same kind of pressures as I was experiencing. There was also something about the intensity of the transference which Dr Z. expected to be too much for one person. Miss K. expected this too, so I knew I must keep firmly to my own personal and professional boundaries, holding on to the familiar framework of analysis, and expect a severe testing-out. In this sense I was forewarned.

Another warning cue was evident in the patient being so compliantly good for my benefit. She was careful not to step over any of the more obvious boundaries, the transgression of which had been such a feature in her previous therapy. As already indicated, she never telephoned; she was always ready to leave at the end of each session; there was no asking for extra contact or any manipulation for this. However, as I listened beyond her compliance, I sensed this to be seductive in order to please, and that it might be an unconscious reminder to me of her need for firmness.

Miss K. seemed never to have experienced anyone prepared, or able, to stand up to her manipulative pressures. It was therefore not surprising that she regarded herself as having something uncontrollable about her. She was still in search of a containing relationship able to withstand these pressures from her. I felt, therefore, that my task was primarily to be that of surviving her manipulations of me, in whatever form these were to come. If I could do that I believed something could be achieved.

My original offer was restricted to twice a week, in order to give me a chance to see how Miss K. and I managed in her sessions. I also needed to decide whether I could realistically risk offering her more intensive therapy, bearing in mind the short time available for her to have therapy in this country. However, once I sensed there was sufficient ego-strength in this patient, and that she was not poised on the edge of an uncontainable regression, I decided she could use analysis.

Feeling intruded upon and/or manipulated

By using two-way trial identification, I was able to learn a lot about Miss K.'s experience of intrusiveness in relationships. For instance, when I listened to my feelings 'in the shoes' of the previous therapist, I picked up an impression of being massively intruded upon by the patient. Dr Z. had frequently been contacted out of session times, and he had agreed to extra sessions. He had also allowed the patient to visit him socially. The patient therefore had an image of a therapist who could be invaded, manipulated and seduced.

Likewise, by trial-identifying with the patient, I could recognize that Miss K. must have been similarly subjected to unmanageable intrusion and manipulation; and it was likely that her previous experience of therapy would have confirmed her worst fears about herself. It was inevitable that these issues would be around with me too.

My role in relation to the acting out

On many occasions Miss K. made me feel helpless, in relation to her acting out – around and against the analysis. Whenever I felt inclined to restrain this by interpretation (as I might with other patients), my trial identification regularly alerted me to the likelihood that she would see me as trying to control her. Her life had been full of other people trying to run her life, so I felt it would be counter-productive if I took on a role which she could realistically see as similar or the same.

I was also alerted by her initial compliance in the analysis, to expect that she was splitting off a healthier but disowned non-compliance. If this were so, that protesting would probably continue to be expressed outside of her relationship to me until we had adequately understood her need to use these defensive ways of relating to me.

I was faced with an acute technical dilemma. I could, of course, still interpret the acting out. Furthermore, I could interpret (in terms of transference) any misunderstanding of my motives for that interpreting, if she assumed I was trying to control her just like everyone else. However, when I did interpret in this way it had little effect. Instead, I had to accept finding myself a helpless witness to the analysis being constantly threatened, perhaps even destroyed, through the various attempts at alternative treatment which were set in motion around it. I knew that it would not help the patient if my motive for trying to control her acting out was mainly in order to reduce my own feelings of discomfort. I also knew that nothing would be gained by getting her to comply with any covert directiveness in my intepretations, aimed at controlling her. That could only result in a facade of change, arrived at falsely. This debate with myself helped me to adopt a different stance in the analysis.

I felt that Miss K. had her own unconscious need for this acting out, chiefly to have a real experience of my letting her run her own life without interference or intrusion from me. I learned to be watchful for any wish of my own to direct her life, whether through word or attitude or manner of expression – however indirectly. We thus came upon her search for space, and her need for me to respect this at whatever cost to me or to my view of myself as analyst.

I had to learn to be ready to accept being made to feel professionally impotent, without having to counter this by attempts to prove otherwise. Only time could tell whether this would be effective or not. I was therefore relieved to find, later in the analysis, that I could resume my interpretation of her unconscious motives behind this acting out, without this becoming a re-enactment of the manipulation of her by others.

Splitting of the transference

During the early part of the analysis Miss K.'s former therapist, like her father, had been persistently idealized. Later, Miss K. came to see for herself that, in important ways, she had not been helped either by her former therapist or by her father because of the lack of boundaries in each relationship. For a while, this awareness led to a shift in the earlier idealization of Dr Z. She then began to idealize her relationship with me, apparently still accepting the boundaries which I adhered to. That idealization of me in the transference could only be modified through my steady interpretation of the patient's acting out, as her disowned attacks upon me, which unconsciously she expected me to be unable to cope with.

From the start, Miss K. appeared to be using her analysis. I thought she was glad of the opportunity to experience a relationship in which there was a clear framework. Meanwhile she was actively attacking the analysis through her acting out against it. Consciously she was not aware of this as an attack, but the unconscious intent became abundantly clear.

As the analysis continued, Miss K. presented me with one alternative treatment after another, each already entered into or set-up. Rather than being put into a position of trying to influence her, concerning these alternative treatments, I chose to go along with her decisions about these – being careful not to evaluate them.

My survival of this testing out gradually emerged in contrast to the background of advice from others. Miss K.'s appreciation of my part in her recovery became apparent quite suddenly during the final period of her analysis, when she was coming five times a week – knowing exactly when she would be leaving England. My survival had opened up a neutral space for her in which she could experiment with how she felt, and how she really wished to be.

For the first time, Miss. K did not have to comply with someone else's wishes. The potency of this was surprising. She was at first incredulous that I had really been able to withstand her pressures on me, which were aimed at making me become directive and controlling of her like everyone else in her life. She then began to relax into a new calm. She had discovered something of vital significance. Her life could be her own, and she did not have to spend all her life proving this. The long-term effects of that realization can be measured by feed-back from the patient, three years later, described in the follow-up below.

Winnicott's notion of the 'Use of an Object'

From the experience of this analysis, the patient and I each learned much. The patient arrived at a real awareness of my separateness, external to her and not controlled by her. She could therefore begin to discover within herself a comparable separateness from me, and from others. She also discovered the creative potential of a relationship-space wherein she could arrive at a new freedom to be herself.

To this end the patient needed me to have an independent reality of my own, and for her to discover this in her own way. It would not have been enough for her if I had just been a passive container for her projections. She needed the assurance, which only experience could give her, that I had my own capacity to survive her attacks and that I did not need her to protect me from them.

I in my turn discovered more about the importance of *space* in a relationship, and I began to appreciate the clinical importance of Winnicott's concept of 'the use of an object' (Winnicott 1971:Chapter 6). Miss K. had been able to make creative use of her own destructiveness, in order to discover that the survival of the other was not dependent upon her.

Once Miss K. had discovered that the other could exist and survive, as an entity in its own right, she was able to discover the possibility of a real separateness. She did not have to remain for ever merged with her mother (or another). Nor did she always have to preserve the person she was relating to, and trying to be separate from, by constantly re-directing her destructive feelings onto others or against herself. It was by inwardly (in phantasy) 'destroying' me as analyst, and the analysis, through her acting out that this patient could eventually discover my otherness from her. She had anticipated either collapse or retaliation, as the only imaginable responses to those aspects of herself which she had come to regard as uncontrollable, and therefore assumed to be omnipotently dangerous.

Winnicott says of this:

> 'At the point of development that is under survey the subject is creating the object in the sense of finding externality itself, and it has to be added that this experience depends on the object's capacity to survive. (It is important that "survive", in this context, means "not retaliate".) If it is in an analysis that these matters are taking place, then the analyst, the analytic technique, and the analytic setting all come in as surviving or not surviving the patient's destructive attacks.'
>
> (Winnicott 1971:91)

I was often tempted to interpret, just to reassure myself that I was still able to think and to function in the session when things seemed most chaotic, but I had to learn to refrain. However, once the acting out had subsided it became possible to interpret this without a sense of wishing to control the patient. Much of the patient's understanding of her acting out was therefore arrived at retrospectively, rather than at the time. It was reassuring to find that Winnicott had written of this too:

> 'The analyst feels like interpreting, but this can spoil the process, and for the patient can seem like a kind of self-defence, the analyst parrying the patient's attack. Better to wait till after the phase is over, and then discuss with the patient what has been happening.'
>
> (Winnicott 1971:92)

It was only with hindsight that I could understand where I had been in this analysis, and why. When, in the end, the patient was able to realize I had continued to survive her attacks upon the analysis, and upon me, she began to discover it was safe for her to become more fully alive in herself. When she ended, she left her analysis freely. This time she left looking forward, not back.

Follow-up

I was very cautious about the possibility of Miss K. writing to me after the end of her analysis. She had already shown how she had used letters in order to hold onto Dr Z., after ending that therapy. However, I also felt that Miss K. should have some way in which she could let me know what she was doing with her life, rather than imagine that her separation from me could only be dealt with by some artificial, almost surgical, cut-off from me. It was therefore agreed that she could write to me some time after she had been through the initial stages of coping with her leaving.

Miss K. wrote me a 'progress report' after four months. Three months later she was passing through London and asked to see me for a single session. I agreed to this. The person who then came to see me was quite different from the patient who had been in analysis with me. She had lost a significant amount of weight, but this was the least of the changes in her. She had a new poise about her. She had been through various personal difficulties, including a relationship disappointment, which previously would have thrown her back to the use of food for revenge and self-comfort. She had not resorted to any of those old ways of escape from conflict. She had dealt with the problems of life with a new maturity.

Miss K. had also come across people from her past, closely linked with her family, who had tried to get her back into the vicious circle of regarding marriage as the only meaningful goal in life, with losing weight to that end as an associated goal. This time she had found enough confidence in herself to be content to make something of her own life in her own way, whether or not this resulted in marriage. She had really begun to find ways of becoming her own self. She had outgrown the former dependence upon her mother and upon her sister and brother-in-law.

Her last comment to me, before she left, was that she had only become able to deal with her weight problem once she had begun to see herself differently. Before, her weight used to express a self which she had assumed to be ugly and unlovable. Feeling different about herself *inwardly* she could now allow herself to express that difference *outwardly* in how she looked. She looked good.

Three years later Miss K. let me know how she had continued to benefit from her analysis. Her new-found confidence in herself had remained with her, and she was finding new satisfactions in life. She had re-discovered the creative side of herself and was beginning once again to sing and to paint. She had developed a full and fulfilling life, and was finding herself able to sustain a close and mutually respecting relationship with a man. Incidentally, too, she had regained a normal weight having lost about sixty pounds since leaving her analysis. The strength and wish for this had come from within. She had achieved this for herself.

Note

1. Although this chapter follows on naturally from the preceding chapter, the work described was done before I had formulated my thoughts on the processes of internal supervision (described in Chapter Two). The reader will be able to recognize that I am here just beginning to find my way towards that.

10

Theory re-discovered

'We shall not cease from exploration
And the end of all our exploring
Will be to arrive where we started
And know the place for the first time.'
(T.S. Eliot: 'Little Gidding')

This book has been about psychoanalytic technique rather than theory. In particular it has been about using internal supervision, and trial identification with the patient, to enable us to distinguish better what helps the analytic process from what hinders it. I have therefore expected a lot from the reader, either to be already familiar with psychoanalytic theory or to be patient while the threads of this emerge from the clinical examples.

Although I have emphasized the therapeutic use of not-knowing, I do not want to give the impression that analytic therapy can be undertaken by learning from the patient alone. A therapist has to be 'held' by the structure provided by theory, and by familiarity with his own unconscious, if he is not to become overwhelmed by a patient's pathology or be retreating into 'head-sight' to avoid being overwhelmed.

For those already well versed in psychoanalytic theory, it will have been clear that much of the work described in this book would have been impossible had the therapist or analyst not been familiar with the complex processes of the unconscious: the mechanisms of defence, the dynamics of growth and development, and the various forms of unconscious inter-action that can occur in any relationship.

Because unconscious speaks to unconscious it is essential that a therapist should have maximal access to this deepest level of interactive communication via his own unconscious responses to the patient. It is for this reason that analysts and therapists have to be analysed; and it is that experience, combined with a knowledge of theory, that helps most to make sense of a therapist's unconscious resonance to what is being communicated by the patient. Without personal analysis there is a limit to how much therapeutic use can be made of these elusive levels of unconscious communication.

Nevertheless, there are numbers of talented social workers, counsellors and others, who demonstrate that (with the help of good supervision) they are able to make valuable use of their knowledge of psychodynamic theory. The therapeutic con-tribution of that work, even though it is different from psychotherapy, should not be discounted. It should be more readily acknowledged and encouraged.

I have tried to illustrate how patients lead the therapist back to what he already knows – or further on to what he still has to find and understand. The essential factor in this process lies in the therapist's willingness to be led by the patient: he has to recognize when he is being prompted and cued, unconsciously supervised or having aspects of himself mirrored by the patient. In ways like this, the therapist not only re-discovers theory; he also discovers how to follow the analytic process. Winnicott says of this:

> 'Analysis is not only a technical exercise. It is something that we become able to do when we have reached a stage in acquiring a basic technique. What we become able to do enables us to co-operate with the patient in following the *process*, that which in each patient has its own pace and which follows its own course; all the important features of this process derive from the patient and not from ourselves as analysts.'
>
> (Winnicott 1958:278)

Unfortunately, even though every student analyst or therapist is taught to follow the patient and not to lead, many still become too sure; and this tendency often remains after qualification. What may then develop is a style of interpreting which is more a matter of *telling* the patient than of *finding out with* the patient. The contrast here is between analytic work which becomes dogmatic and that which draws upon the patient's own creativity.

Many therapists quote examples of their clinical work in which they have made statements that imply a surprising degree of certainty. 'I told the patient...', 'I then showed the patient that...' and 'no doubt this was because...': all are phrases which are common in the literature. Why is this so? Is it because psychoanalytic theory has become so refined, and the body of shared clinical experience so convincing, that analysts can now work with a theoretical sureness that would have been impossible to the early explorers in this field of the human psyche? Or is there something else here to do with a need to appear competent, perhaps linked with a self-expectation that one should know? Might there, sometimes, also be an unconscious collusion between the patient's search for certainty and a clinical stance of the therapist appearing to offer it?

I find these questions troubling. If theory is to remain alive, rather than being repeatedly demonstrated in relation to each patient, there has to be adequate room for the patient to play with what is around in the session. It is important, therefore, that the therapist does not dominate the analytic work or monopolize insight in the therapy.

If too much certainty is employed by a therapist, this offers a patient what appears to be a short-cut to 'knowing'. The dangers here are that insight is intellectualized, that understanding rests on a false basis, and that the therapist appears more all-knowing than anyone really can be. There are no short-cuts to pyschoanalytic experience. There is no other path to it than patience, the therapist holding onto the caution of still not-knowing – alongside the dawning sense of beginning to understand.

When a patient is ready to recognize the unconscious implications of what is being communicated, or being experienced in the session, the therapist can begin to draw the patient's attention to the evidence that points to possible unconscious meaning. For this reason, I prefer to speak more in terms of 'maybe' or 'perhaps', which I believe to be the natural language of potential space. I have also suggested that therapists should develop the art of finding a half-way step toward insight. This does not fore-close on the patient's options, and it allows mental space for him to play with the therapist's comments when these are offered tentatively. They can then be altered, added to or dismissed – by patient or therapist. Instead of insight being *given* to the patient it can be *discovered* by patient and therapist together. Interpretation does not then become an impingement.

Of course there are many occasions when the therapist should be more sure than merely tentative; when he can offer interpretation with conviction based on the work already done with the patient, or when he has to deal with clear unconscious resistance from the patient. But that sureness of interpretation, if it is to be personal to the patient (not a cliché-response), still has to be arrived at from the patient's own cues and not just from being familiar with psychoanalytic theory. The most obvious time when a firm understanding is necessary is when a patient feels in crisis and needs containment.

A patient in ferment is like a wine in the making. There is life in the fermentation, to contain which the container must be able to respond to the pressures of growth. Each patient unconsciously looks for a therapist who can be in touch with that growth, be responsive to it, and able to be firm without being rigid. Borrowed insight can never serve that function. What is needed, but is not always offered by the therapist, is insight that is discovered with this patient in this session of this therapy.

No-one can *make* another person grow. One can only inhibit growth or enable it. Therapists therefore need to understand the processes of growth and the dynamics of what inhibits this. Trial identification will often expose those times when a therapist is blocking a patient's experience, and the opportunity for new growth. Often, this blocking is caused by a therapist pre-empting the patient with premature interpretation, implicitly directing the patient to proceed along the anticipated lines of regression, or transference etc., as already extensively described in the literature.

There is a temptation, rooted in the acquired knowledge of psychoanalytic theory, for analysts and therapists to try to mastermind the analytic process rather than to follow it. As with infants, the process of analytic growth has its own impetus. Infants whose natural growth is not interfered with usually wean themselves, and can toilet train themselves too, *when they are ready*. Patients will likewise often resist a therapist's premature application of theoretical knowledge, and pre-conceived ideas about them, in order to reinstate the necessary 'period of hesitation' (Winnicott 1958:53). Without the space created by this hesitation there can be no room for analytic discovery or play. With it there is room, in every analysis and therapy treatment, for theory to be re-discovered and renewed.

I have described clinical issues as I have found them. I have offered my own understanding of these, but I make no claim for the rightness of how I handled them. The extended clinical examples have been recorded, as far as possible, as they happened. They are offered for learning from and for teaching; they are not meant to be used in any way as a model for others. The reader will find that I have often failed to follow my own ideas on technique. This is partly because my thinking about technique has been influenced by my reflection on the many things that I wish I had done differently. It is also easier to be wise after the event than when caught up in the immediacy of the session itself.

I leave much unanswered; but to have recognized some of the questions is at least a beginning.

> 'I am a part of all that I have met;
> Yet all experience is an arch wherethro'
> Gleams that untravell'd world, whose margin fades
> For ever and for ever when I move.'
>
> (Tennyson: *Ulysses*, 1842)

Appendix I

Knowing and not-knowing: Winnicott and Bion

From Winnicott

'An infant is merged with the mother.... A change, however, comes with the end of merging.... The mother seems to know that the infant has a new capacity, that of giving a signal so that she can be guided towards meeting the infant's needs. It could be said that if now she knows too well what the infant needs, this is magic and forms no basis for an object relationship.... We find this subtlety appearing clearly in the transference in our analytic work. It is very important, except when the patient is regressed to earliest infancy and to a state of merging, that the analyst shall *not* know the answers except in so far as the patient gives the clues. The analyst gathers the clues and makes the interpretations, and it often happens that patients fail to give the clues, making certain thereby that the analyst can do nothing. This limitation of the analyst's power is important to the patient, just as the analyst's power is important, represented by the interpretation that is right and that is made at the right moment, and that is based on the clues and the unconscious co-operation of the patient who is supplying the material which builds up and justifies the interpretation. In this way the student analyst sometimes does better analysis than he will do in a few years' time when he knows more. When he has had several patients he begins to find it irksome to go as slowly as the patient is going, and he begins to make interpretations based not on material supplied on that particular day by the patient but on his own accumulated knowledge or his adherence for the time being to a particular group of ideas. This is of no use to the patient. The analyst may appear to be very clever, and the patient may express admiration, but in the end the correct interpretation is a trauma, which the patient has to reject, because it is not his.'

(Winnicott 1965b:50-1)

'What I have to say... is extremely simple. Although it comes out of my psychoanalytical experience I would not say that it could have come out of my psychoanalytical experience of two decades ago, because I would not then have had the technique to make possible the transference movements that I wish to describe. For instance, it is only in recent years that I have become able to wait and wait for the natural evolution of the transference arising out of the patient's growing trust in the psychoanalytic technique and setting, and to avoid breaking up this natural process by making interpretations.... If only we can wait, the patient arrives at understanding creatively and with immense joy, and I now enjoy this joy more than I used to enjoy the sense of having been clever. I think I interpret mainly to let the patient know the limits of my understanding. The principle is that it is the patient and only the patient who has the answers.'

(Winnicott 1971:86-7)

From Bion

'Discard your memory; discard the future tense of your desire; forget them both, both what you knew and what you want, to leave space for a new idea. A thought, an idea unclaimed, may be floating around the room searching for a home. Amongst these may be one of your own which seems to turn up from your insides, or one from outside yourself, namely, from the patient.'

(Bion 1980:11)

'Instead of trying to bring a brilliant, intelligent, knowledgeable light to bear on obscure problems, I suggest we bring to bear a diminution of the "light" – a penetrating beam of darkness; a reciprocal of the searchlight.... The darkness would be so absolute that it would achieve a luminous, absolute vacuum. So that, if any object existed, however faint, it would show up very clearly. Thus, a very faint light would become visible in maximum conditions of darkness.'

(Bion 1974:37)

'Psycho-analysts must be able to tolerate the differences or the difficulties of the analysand long enough to recognise what they are. If psycho-analysts are to be able to interpret what the analysand says, they must have a great capacity for tolerating their analysands' statements without rushing to the conclusion that they know the interpretations. This is what I think Keats meant when he said that Shakespeare must have been able to tolerate "negative capability".'

(Bion 1974:72)

'...*Negative Capability*, that is, when a man is capable of being in uncertainties, mysteries, doubts, without any irritable reaching after fact and reason.'

(John Keats: Letter to George and Thomas Keats, 21 December 1817)

Appendix II

The issues of confidentiality and of exposure by the therapist

There are a number of important issues to be considered, around the question of confidentiality, before we can think of using clinical material for the purposes of shared learning about psychoanalysis and psychotherapy.

It is generally accepted that patients in analysis and therapy have an absolute right to expect total confidentiality. They must, therefore, always be protected from exposure in any clinical material that is used for teaching or publication. So, every analyst and therapist is faced with the ethical question 'Whether or not to publish, or to use for teaching, clinical material that others might be able to learn from?'

There are various ways of dealing with this dilemma. We could try to ban any shared learning, in the name of preserving a total confidentiality; but it is doubtful that we could help our patients even as much as we sometimes do, if we were unable to learn from the work of others in the field.

We could insist that we never publish, or use for teaching purposes, anything from a patient's treatment without permission from that patient. However, asking a patient about possible publication, during the course of therapy or analysis, introduces an intrusive factor into the analytic process. Some patients are unable to cope with this 'rocking the boat' of the analytic experience, and it will always rock it. We cannot always assess correctly when it is right to ask for that permission from a patient. It may never be right.

We could, instead, confine ourselves to clinical material from patients who have finished their treatment, asking then for permission to publish. This too is not without its problems. When patients leave therapy it is their right to be left free from continuing contact with the therapist. One would not want to interfere with the achieved separateness that is aimed for at the close of therapy or analysis. Moreover, such continuing contact can get in the way of a patient's freedom to return for further treatment.

One safeguard could be to wait a minimum period (some say ten years) after treatment is concluded before publishing any clinical material; but this slows down the process of shared learning. Another way to preserve patients' freedom, and their right to absolute confidentiality, is to use clinical material from other people's work with patients. This has many advantages; but it can shift the burden of the problem onto others. It can also be a way of therapists preserving themselves from the critical assessment by others which they may *need* in order to improve their understanding.

For this reason I have decided not to hide my work from examination by others; and I have been influenced in this by my impression that clinical presentations (spoken or published) too often show the presenter in a good light. Analysts and therapists do not so readily share their failures, but I think that more can be gained by all when some are prepared to do so.

I have also used disguised examples from clinical work that I have supervised. I trust that no student therapist will feel a sense of injury from this sharing of their struggles to become better therapists. Having decided to publish, I have dealt with the issues of confidentiality and permission for publication with careful consideration of the over-all situation for each patient concerned, and for those I have supervised.

I hope that the clinical vignettes in this book, and the longer clinical presentations, will provide useful learning material. There were certainly many lessons for me contained in these examples. If others can learn from the self-exposure involved I believe that this will have been worthwhile.

I cannot speak for the patients concerned or for the people I have supervised. Those who have given their permission for publication will, I trust, recognize the care with which I preserve their anonymity. I wish to believe that those others, from whom (for whatever reason) I have preferred not to ask permission, will not recognize themselves. If any patient or student does, I trust that they can still preserve their own freedom not to have themselves identified by anyone else.

I hope that this book will not deter any patient from seeking analytic help. Rather, it is my wish that it may help to promote an analytic atmosphere in which patients can expect to be better listened to.

I am indebted to all those I have worked with, for what I have learned from them, without which this book could never have been written. If patients (or those I have supervised) have gained as much from the clinical encounter as I have, I hope they may be glad that I have considered it to be worth sharing some of this with others.

References

ALEXANDER, F. (1954) Some Quantitative Aspects of Psychoanalytic Technique. *Journal of the American Psychoanalytic Association* 2:685-701.
BALINT, M. (1952) *Primary Love and Psycho-Analytic Technique*. London: Tavistock Publications.
— (1968) *The Basic Fault: Therapeutic Aspects of Regression*. London: Tavistock Publications.
BION, W.R. (1967a) Notes on Memory and Desire. *Psychoanalytic Forum* 2:271-80.
— (1967b) *Second Thoughts*. New York: Aronson.
— (1974) *Brazilian Lectures 1*. Rio de Janeiro: Imago Editora.
— (1975) *Brazilian Lectures 2*. Rio de Janeiro: Imago Editora.
— (1980) *Bion in New York and São Paulo*. Ed. F. Bion. Perthshire: Clunie Press.
CASEMENT, P.J. (1969) The Setting of Limits: a Belief in Growth. *Case Conference*, 16(7):267-71.
— (1973) The Supervisory Viewpoint. In W.F. Finn (ed.) *Family Therapy in Social Work: Conference Papers*. London: Family Welfare Association.
— (1982) Some Pressures on the Analyst for Physical Contact during the Re-Living of an Early Trauma. *International Review of Psycho-Analysis* 9:279-86.
— (1984) The Reflective Potential of the Patient as Mirror to the Therapist. In J.O. Raney (ed.) *Listening and Interpreting: the Challenge of the Work of Robert Langs*. New York: Aronson.
CHESTERTON, G.K. (1908) *Orthodoxy*. Reprinted (1961). London: Fontana Books.
DOUCET, P. and LAURIN, C. (eds) (1971) *Problems of Psychosis*. Amsterdam: Excerpta Medica.
EISSLER, K.R. (1953) The Effect of the Structure of the Ego on Psychoanalytic Technique. *Journal of the American Psychoanalytic Association* 1:104-43.

ELIOT, T.S. (1935) 'Little Gidding'. In *Four Quartets*. (1949) London: Faber & Faber.

EPSTEIN, L. and FEINER, A.H. (eds) (1979) *Countertransference*. New York: Aronson.

FINN, W.R. (ed.) (1973) *Family Therapy in Social Work: Conference Papers*. London: Family Welfare Association.

FLEISS, R. (1942) The Metapsychology of the Analyst. *Psychoanalytic Quarterly* 11:211-27.

FOX, R.P. (1984) The Principle of Abstinence Reconsidered. *International Review of Psycho-Analysis* 11:227-36.

FREUD, A. (1937) *The Ego and Mechanisms of Defence*. London: Hogarth Press.

FREUD, S. (1900) The Interpretation of Dreams. *Standard Edition* 5. London: Hogarth Press and the Institute of Psycho-Analysis.

— (1910) The Future Prospects of Psychotherapy. *Standard Edition* 11.

— (1914/1915) Observations of Transference-Love. *Standard Edition* 12.

— (1915) The Unconscious. *Standard Edition* 14.

— (1927) The Future of an Illusion. *Standard Edition* 21.

— (1933/1934) New Introductory Lectures. *Standard Edition* 22.

GIOVACCHINI, P.L, (ed.) (1975) *Tactics and Techniques in Psychoanalytic Therapy*, Vol 11. New York: Aronson.

GROTSTEIN, J.S. (1981) *Splitting and Projective Identification*. New York: Aronson.

HEIMANN, P. (1950) On Counter-Transference. *International Journal of Psycho-Analysis* 31:81-4.

KERNBERG, O. (1965) Notes on Countertransference. *Journal of the American Psychoanalytic Association* 13:38-56.

KING, P. (1978) Affective Response of the Analyst to the Patient's Communications. *International Journal of Psycho-Analysis* 59:329-34.

KLEIN, M. (1946) Notes on some Schizoid Mechanisms. In J. Riviere (ed.) *Developments in Pycho-Analysis*. London: Hogarth Press (1952).

— (1952) Some Theoretical Conclusions Regarding the Emotional Life of the Infant. In J. Riviere (ed.) *Developments in Pycho-Analysis*. London: Hogarth Press (1952).

KRIS, E. (1950) On Preconscious Mental Processes. *Psychoanalytic Quarterly* 19:540-60.

LANGS, R.J. (1978) *The Listening Process*. New York: Aronson.

LAPLANCHE, J. and PONTONALIS, J-B. (1973) *The Language of Psychoanalysis*. London: Hogarth Press.

LEITES, N. (1977) Transference Interpretations Only?. *International Journal of Psycho-Analysis* 58:275-87.

LITTLE, M. (1951) Counter-Transference and the Patient's Response to it. *International Journal of Psycho-Analysis* 32:32-40.

MATTE BLANCO, I. (1975) *The Unconscious as Infinite Sets*. London: Duckworth.

MILNER, M. (1952) Aspects of Symbolism in Comprehension of the Not-Self. *International Journal of Psycho-Analysis* 33:181-95.

MONEY-KYRLE, R. (1956) Normal Counter-Transference and some of its Deviations. *International Journal of Psycho-Analysis* 37:360-66.

OGDEN, T. (1982) *Projective Identification and Psychotherapeutic Technique.* New York: Aronson.

ORR, D.W. (1954) Transference and Countertransference: a Historical Survey. *Journal of the American Psychoanalytic Association* 2:621-70.

RACKER, H. (1968) *Transference and Counter-Transference.* London: Hogarth Press.

RANEY, J.O. (ed.) (1984) *Listening and Interpreting: The Challenge of the Work of Robert Langs.* New York: Aronson.

RAYNER, E. (1981) Infinite Experiences, Affects and the Characteristics of the Unconscious. *International Journal of Psycho-Analysis* 62:403-12.

REICH, A. (1951) On Counter-Transference. *International Journal of Psycho-Analysis* 32:25-31.

REIK, T. (1937) *Surprise and the Psychoanalyst.* New York: E.P. Dutton & Co.

RIVIERE, J. (1952) (ed.) *Developments in Psycho-Analysis.* London: Hogarth Press.

ROSENFELD, H. (1965) *Psychotic States.* London: Hogarth Press.

— (1971) Contribution to the Psychopathology of Psychotic States. In P. Doucet and C. Laurin (eds) *Problems of Pychosis.* Amsterdam: Excerpta Medica.

SANDLER, J. (1976) Countertransference and Role-Responsiveness. *International Review of Psycho-Analysis* 3:43-7.

— (1983) Reflections on some Relations between Psychoanalytic Concepts and Psychoanalytic Practice. *International Journal of Psycho-Analysis* 64:35-45.

— DARE, C. and HOLDER, A. (1973) *The Patient and the Analyst: The Basis of the Psychoanalytic Process.* London: George Allen & Unwin.

SEARLES, H. (1975) The Patient as Therapist to his Analyst. In P.L. Giovacchini (ed.) *Tactics and Techniques in Psychoanalytic Therapy*, Vol II. New York: Aronson.

SEGAL, H. (1964). *Introduction to the Work of Melanie Klein.* London: Heinemann.

STERBA, R. (1934) The Fate of the Ego in Analytic Therapy. *International Journal of Psycho-Analysis* 15:117-26.

STRACHEY, J. (1934) The Nature of the Therapeutic Interaction of Psychoanalysis. *International Journal of Psycho-Analysis.* 15:127-59.

TOWER, L.E. (1956) Countertransference. *Journal of the American Psychoanalytic Association* 4:224-55.

WANGH, M. (1962) The 'Evocation of a Proxy': A Psychological Maneuver, Its Use as a Defense, Its Purpose and Genesis. *The Psychoanalytic Study of the Child* 17:451-69.

WINNICOTT, D.W. (1958) *Collected Papers: Through Paediatrics to Psycho-Analysis.* London: Tavistock Publications.

— (1965a) *The Family and Individual Development.* London: Tavistock Publications.

— (1965b) *Maturational Processes and the Facilitating Environment*. London: Hogarth Press.

— (1970) Fear of Breakdown. *International Review of Psycho-Analysis* [1974] 1:103-07.

— (1971) *Playing and Reality*. London: Tavistock Publications.

Name index

Subject index

abandonment, sense of 89-90; *see also*
   rejection
absence: of feelings 79; of mother,
   re-experienced 89-91, 128-29, 158;
   theme of 119, 158
abstracting themes 8-9, 11, 37-8, 41-2,
   44, 112, 117; *see also* interpretation;
   themes
abstinence 171, 189; *see also* flexibility
acting out 191, 204; against analysis
   202-06, 210-14; of countertransference 60-3, 85-8; interpretation
   of 191, 211; toleration of 190-91,
   210-12
action as communication *see* cushion;
   impact; lateness
action, discharge through 49-51
activity: patient's, as defense 80;
   therapist's level of 58, 122, 135
actualization 75, 201-02; *see also* role-
   responsiveness
addictive avoidance 133, 194-95; *see
   also* eating; medication
adolescence, need for firmness in 23-4,
   26; *see also* developmental needs
advice: giving 186, 199; of supervisor
   32; *see also* deflection; leading
affective communication, projective
   identification as 80-2; *see also*
   projective identification
aggression, therapist's defense against
   18-19; *see also* communication;
   impact; resistance
aggressor, identification with 83-5,
   89-91, 96-7, 127; *see also*
   communication; impact
alertness, therapist's lack of 63; *see also*
   attention; lapses; mistakes
alternative therapist, looking for 41,

201-02, 211; *see also* splitting
ambiguity: in communication 35, 113;
   and symmetry, 38; *see also* symmetry
analysis: decision to offer 208-10;
   different styles of 21, 27; and
   nursing triad 22-3; self- 35; wild 21
anonymity 88, 226; *see also* boundaries;
   confidentiality
anxiety: as cue 157; deepest, as focus
   for interpretation 45-6; history of
   59-60; medication for 141; most
   urgent, as focus for interpretation
   48; therapist's 58-9; unmanageable
   2, 129-30, 150; unresolved, need to
   analyse 104
association, free 181, 189
assumptions: based on theory 11;
   premature, therapist's 36; *see also*
   formulation; interpretation; timing
attention: evenly suspended 38; free
   floating 56; lapses in 63-4, 68, 106-
   09, 120; new focus for, as deflection
   49-51, 85-8, 106-07, 111, 115-17,
   119-29, 132-33, 172-74, 187-89; *see
   also* alertness; lapses; listening;
   mistakes
autonomy: patient's 169, 192, 205;
   therapist's 32, 49; *see also*
   boundaries; framework; space
avoidance: of impact 153; of present
   51; of trauma 159; *see also* deflection

babies, death of 78-80
baby, unborn, as threat to mother
   14-16
balance: between closeness and
   distance 30; in listening and
   interpretation 38; quest for 29-30,
   180; therapist's loss of 83, 121; *see*